ALCOHOL IGNITION INTERLOCK PROGRAMS

ELEMENTS AND CONSIDERATIONS TO PREVENT IMPAIRED DRIVING

CRIMINAL JUSTICE, LAW ENFORCEMENT AND CORRECTIONS

Additional books in this series can be found on Nova's website under the Series tab.

Additional e-books in this series can be found on Nova's website under the e-book tab.

CRIMINAL JUSTICE, LAW ENFORCEMENT AND CORRECTIONS

ALCOHOL IGNITION INTERLOCK PROGRAMS

ELEMENTS AND CONSIDERATIONS TO PREVENT IMPAIRED DRIVING

ELISE B. TIESSART
EDITOR

nova publishers
New York

For permission to use material from this book please contact us:
Telephone 631-231-7269; Fax 631-231-8175
Web Site: http://www.novapublishers.com

Library of Congress Cataloging-in-Publication Data

ISBN: 978-1-62948-546-1

Published by Nova Science Publishers, Inc. † New York

CONTENTS

PREFACE

The general topics in the body of this book include program enrollment issues; interlock program ramp-up and expansion; standardization of reporting and information flow; program compliance, noncompliance and interlock removal; linkages to treatment; differences in court-based judicial programs and motor vehicle administered interlock programs; and suggested core elements of interlock programs. The authors believe that the single major difference among panelists interviewed centered on whether interlocks should play a role in the monitoring of court- ordered alcohol abstinence.

Chapter 1 – This report describes an effort to document alcohol ignition interlock programs in the United States in order to highlight those programs or program features that are believed to be best able to serve traffic safety interests. Information has been gathered into this report bearing on important interlock program features together with some recommendations for States to consider as programs are developed. This publication reflects information of the time it was written. Therefore, some statements may be outdated.

Chapter 2 – The purpose of this alcohol ignition interlock toolkit is to provide information about alcohol ignition interlocks and their use to prevent impaired driving. Many States have legislation that requires an alcohol ignition interlock to be placed on the vehicles of Driving While Intoxicated (DWI) offenders.

The toolkit includes sections that address frequently asked questions about interlocks, cost and benefits of ignition interlock programs, research on ignition interlocks, point- counterpoint on ignition interlocks, talking points, and the current use of ignition interlocks by State. The toolkit also addresses issues to consider when putting together an ignition interlock program such as indigent funding, monitoring, and offender compliance.

In: Alcohol Ignition Interlock Programs
Editor: Elise B. Tiessart
ISBN: 978-1-62948-546-1

Chapter 1

KEY FEATURES FOR IGNITION INTERLOCK PROGRAMS*

Paul R. Marques and Robert B. Voas

ABSTRACT

This report describes an effort to document alcohol ignition interlock programs in the United States in order to highlight those programs or program features that are believed to be best able to serve traffic safety interests. Information has been gathered into this report bearing on important interlock program features together with some recommendations for States to consider as programs are developed. This publication reflects information of the time it was written. Therefore, some statements may be outdated.

EXECUTIVE SUMMARY

Background

This report documents features of current interlock programs around the United States. Alcohol ignition interlock devices began to be used more widely in the United States after passage of the 1986 Farr-Davis Driver Safety

* This is an edited, reformatted and augmented version of the National Highway Traffic Safety Administration, U.S. Department of Transportation, DOT HS 811 262, dated March 2010.

Act in California (EMT Group, 1990). That law provided for a pilot test in a few California counties. Soon after, other States began to write legislation that supported use of this technology. As legislation began to grow through the late 1980s, the National Highway Traffic Safety Administration became engaged with an effort to assist the States by publishing certification guidelines (NHTSA, 1992) for the devices that were coming into the marketplace. Those Model Specifications for Breath Alcohol Ignition Interlock Devices (a.k.a. Model Specifications) were restricted to giving advice to States on how to evaluate the adequacy of the *interlock hardware* available for installation, not how to create or manage a program. The Model Specifications served to organize the development of State laws, but other than a companion document (Voas & Marques, 1992) that was published under the same NHTSA contract, there was too little known to give authoritative recommendations about how the interlock laws and programs should be developed. This publication reflects information of the time it was written. Therefore, some statements may be outdated.

In the absence of clear directives from the Federal Government or sufficient experience upon which to guide selection of program features, the interlock manufacturers were often the primary source of expertise available to the States. Accordingly, certain processes that facilitate intrastate communication between divisions of government were missing, and some monitoring functions were dispersed to the private vendors providing the interlock service programs. This sort of haphazard development is not all bad as it has led to some creative program efforts by States, but there comes a time when a more intentional organization of interlock programs is warranted. With the growing sophistication and penetration of interlocks into the problem of managing impaired driving offenders, several program design and management issues would benefit from a central resource for best practice and expert opinion.

Features of Interlock Devices and Programs

Device Characteristics. Ignition interlocks currently in use have four basic elements: (1) a breath alcohol sensor in the vehicle (and a control unit under the hood) that records the driver's blood alcohol concentration (BAC) and can be set to provide a warning if any alcohol is detected and, based on some criterion, such as the NHTSA Model Specifications that recommends the vehicle not start if the BAC is .025 grams per deciliter (g/dL) or higher; (2) a rolling retest system, which requires at least one retest after the vehicle is underway, but in most applications a retest is required every 20 to 30 minutes while driving (the purpose of the retests is to prevent a non-driver from starting the vehicle for a person who has been drinking and also to prevent drinking once the vehicle is underway); (3) a tamper-proof system for mounting the engine part of the unit, which is inspected every 30 to 60 days to preclude circumvention, along with a system to detect hotwiring or other means that bypass the interlock; and (4) a data-recording system that logs the BAC results, test compliance and engine operation, and creates a record to ensure that the offender is actually using the vehicle as expected and not simply parking it while driving another vehicle.

Evidence for Program Effectiveness. There are now about 15 studies of interlock effectiveness in the literature. Evidence from most demonstrate 35to 75-percent effectiveness *while installed on the vehicle*; most studies were statistically controlled but not randomly assigned. A recent meta analysis by Willis, Lybrand, and Bellamy (2004) found that, while installed, the interlock reduced the relative risk of DWI recidivism by 64 percent. Once the interlock is removed from the vehicle, the recidivism rate generally returns to the level of similar offenders who have not installed interlocks. The fact that when the interlock is on the offender's vehicle recidivism is reduced compared to when it is not on the vehicle suggests that it is an effective method for incapacitating the offender.

Barrier to Better Program Effectiveness. A major limitation on the safety impact of interlocks has been the weakness of interlock laws, the reticence of some judges to require use of interlocks and the resistance of offenders to installing them. In addition, some localities lack interlock providers. As a result, in many States with interlock laws, just 10 to 20 percent of offenders eligible for interlock programs install them. As of 2008, the estimated ratio of installed interlocks to DWI arrests across the country is about 1 to 10.

Judicial Versus Administrative Programs. State interlock programs can be divided into those that are primarily administered by the courts and those that are managed by the State licensing authority. There are advantages and disadvantages to each type. The most fundamental difference is that courts have substantial power to enforce the requirement for an interlock by threatening harsher sanctions such as jail if an offender refuses to comply, but not all judges order use of the interlocks. By contrast, administrative programs, managed by the State licensing authorities, have only the power to withhold the driving privilege, but more consistently order their use. There is a growing trend toward hybrid court and administrative programs.

Method

Background Information. For this project, we collected information from several sources bearing on important interlock program features that should be considered when setting implementation policies. The sources included published and unpublished literature, information acquired from key informants via telephone interviews of State officials and program managers, an issues discussion at the 7th Ignition Interlock Symposium in Beaver Creek, Colorado, in 2006; that discussion led to the development of a survey of key informants that was conducted by the International Council on Alcohol, Drugs, and Traffic Safety (ICADTS) Interlock Working Group (IWG). All of this preliminary information culminated in pre-read material in advance of an assembly of an expert panel to discuss and offer views.

Expert Panel. The one-day expert panel convened on October 4, 2007, and was comprised of 28 people selected from around North America. The panel participants' views and expertise represented a spectrum of interests and knowledge about use of ignition interlock devices in the prevention and adjudication of impaired driving offenses (also referred to in this report as DWI, or driving while impaired, offenses). Panelists represented judges, prosecutors, defense attorneys, manufacturers, treatment professionals, State program managers, probation officers, interlock researchers, NHTSA officials and the victim community, which was represented by Mothers Against Drunk Driving (MADD) USA (at the table) and MADD Canada (in written commentary).

The expert panel served as the final step in a process of information sifting, which set the stage for producing this final report summarizing the authors' interpretation of the evidence and commentary, based on the literature review, survey results, and expert panel commentary on programs and procedures. Because there is no formal research available on many of the topics covered in this study, reliance had to be placed on the experiences of program managers, researchers, judges, Government authorities, and vendors to provide the best guide to reasonable answers to questions regarding ignition interlock programs. Opinion or anecdotes often can represent deep wells of experience in a wide variety of program types. Accordingly, the discussion topics selected for the expert panel came from the informed opinions of many and were extracted from many sources. The expert panel provided a useful airing of opinions and, where possible, based either on published evidence or near consensus views of experts, recommendations are provided. The following sections provide an overview of the body of the report. Each topical area is followed by some recommendations and the page number where the topic is discussed more fully. Recommendations regarding key elements and features of ignition interlock programs represent the interpretations of the authors, and reflect input from the expert panel and key informants, as well as other sources.

Overview of Key Features in Interlock Programs

1. Installation and Program Enrollment Issues

Nearly all programs have low enrollment/installation/penetration relative to the annual number of DWI arrests and convictions. Knowing that DWI recidivism is reduced by about 65 percent while interlocks are installed, how can we improve interlock use/enrollment? How long should someone be on a program? How soon after arrest should an interlock be available?

Q: Should first-time DWI offenders be included in interlock programs?

A: Yes. The evidence seems to support interlocks for all offenders (p. 19).

Q: Should full relicensing after a DWI conviction require a period of interlock-controlled driving?

A: Yes. If interlock is refused by offender, an alternative BAC monitoring system should be available as a requirement for license reinstatement (p. 20).

Q: Should the interlock requirement be added to those with hardship or limited licenses? Similarly, should interlock drivers be able to drive without limits or in some cases be issued a limited or hardship license?

A: The interlock is warranted for nearly all alcohol offenders including those on hardship licenses. Once an interlock is installed, some experts believe that it is best to allow unlimited driving. More research is needed to guide the use of limited or hardship licenses with the interlock for certain types of high risk offenders (p.20-21).

Q: How long should suspension/revocation periods extend before interlock eligibility? That is, should there be support for early interlock installation following arrest or conviction? Or should traditional lengthy suspension periods prior to interlock be encouraged?

A: Allowing early entry should probably be encouraged. It seems to be showing promising results in New Mexico, but comparative research is needed (p.21-22).

Q: What is a reasonable duration for interlock programs?

A: The length should reflect the seriousness of the offense (p. 22-23).

2. Interlock Program Ramp-Up and Expansion

Q: What concrete advice can be offered to States ready to start up or make major expansions? How can they learn from the experiences of others?

A: This report lists 22 recommendations to support growth of interlock programs (p.23-26).

Q: What should an interlock program cost offenders?

A: Monthly fee varies from $65 to $90. Installation may cost between $100 and $250 (p.27).

Q: How should programs accommodate low income or indigent offenders?

A: States should make arrangement with vendors to offset some of the program costs for low income offenders (p.27).

Q: What circumvention protections should new programs be attuned to?

A: Each State with an interlock program should adopt a standard to guide its selection of suitable devices. The standard, if based on the Federal Model Specifications, will require that approvable devices have anticircumvention methods, but the interlock program must require that these be active and used (p.28-29).

Q: How should interlock providers (vendors) be managed? Should there be a controlled number of vendors or an open competition in each State?

A: There are a variety of approaches to this by different States. Fewer vendors make it easier to combine data, but whatever the model chosen, the State should monitor vendor performance (p. 29-30).

3. Standardization of Reporting and Information Flow

Q: Communication and information flow is organized haphazardly in many State programs. How can we improve information moving from: private industry to administrators, administrators to courts/probation, courts to offenders, all to each other?

A: This report contains some general and specific suggestions for consideration, and suggests that specifications for program reporting would be useful (p.30-31).

Q: What type of reporting formats from service providers to monitoring authority should be recommended or required?

A: This report includes recommendations in five general areas with several component suggestions under each, including that it is important to adopt clear definitions of all key terms so that information across different vendors can be understood to mean the same thing. Currently, they do not. It is recommended also that a consistent frequency of reporting to the monitoring authority be established (p. 31-34).

Q: Should there be a minimal vehicle use requirement to guard against the offender parking the vehicle and waiting out a required interlock period?

A: Some protocol should be established. Currently, the odometer reading is used, but it is also possible to examine the number of BAC tests each month to assure adequate vehicle use (p. 34).

4. Program Compliance, Noncompliance, and Interlock Removal

Q: Should there be different consequences for different types of noncompliance? Procedural violations and circumvention

attempts differ from BAC levels recorded as locked out starts in the data log file. Should States regard these differently?

A: Three types of noncompliance are discussed; repeated BAC lockouts, procedural failures such as not performing a retest when required and circumvention as indicated by starting the vehicle without taking a breath test. Circumventions that involve altering the device should result in a significant sanction, such as more stringent monitoring with a monitoring bracelet or house arrest (p. 34).

Q: How should States address issues of BAC lockouts?

A: BAC lockouts are predictive of future post-interlock recidivism (Marques, Tippetts, Voas, & Beirness, 2001; Marques, Tippetts, & Voas, 2003b; Marques, Voas, & Tippetts, 2003). Lockout rates decline with time on the interlock as offenders learn to adapt to them. States should have an active monitoring effort with warnings for those who have repeated lockouts (p. 35).

Q: Should there be different performance expectations placed on the offender as a function of time in the program? Should the monitoring authority's definition of "compliance" become stricter after months of practice using an interlock?

A: It is recommended that there be some performance standard that in the last 3 to 6 months requires regular vehicle use with no lockouts. (p. 36-37).

Q: Should there be extensions on interlock programs for some offenders with repeated lockout BAC tests? What should trigger an extension in the interlock program?

A: Currently, several States (Colorado, West Virginia, Michigan, Pennsylvania, and Virginia) have provisions for extending time on the interlock for repeated BAC lock-outs. Providing for extensions of offenders who appear to be unable to control their drinking appears important, but is dependent on good records of interlock performance. (p.37).

Q: Now that BAC monitoring of DWI offenders is possible via the interlock breath test record, should programs require a demonstration that a driver is no longer experiencing alcohol

lockouts before ending the interlock requirement and reissuing an unrestricted driver's license?

A: DWI offenders should be required to demonstrate 3 to 6 months of alcohol-free driving before reissuance of an unrestricted license (p. 37).

Q: How can we reconcile the core design of interlocks (to prevent impaired driving) with the desire of some court programs to use interlocks as an abstinence monitoring tool? What are the implications of these different philosophies for dealing with BAC lockouts or program extensions?

A: Differences between those who emphasize the importance of maintaining the interlock to control driving and judges who order abstinence and use interlocks to monitor compliance, were not fully resolved. One suggestion was to institute a series of milder but escalating penalties, such as an extension of time on the interlock, or alternatively devising separate programs if courts want an interlock to serve as an abstinence monitoring tool (p. 38-39).

Q: Is the development of standards for two types of programs the way to resolve this abstinence versus graded attainment of drinking control?

A: There is no clear evidence to suggest better outcomes would accrue with either path. This is an area where more research may help to evaluate the pros and cons of each approach (p 39-40).

5. Linkage to Treatment

Q: The evidence shows that many treatment interventions linked to DWI sanctions have only a modest impact and are not systematically structured, monitored, evaluated, or applied. Does the interlock, with its data record of BAC tests, hold promise for improving the effectiveness of DWI treatment interventions? Or should these remain separate parts of the remediation process?

A: It is recommended that States integrate interlock and treatment programs (p.40).

Q: If the government demands abstinence, does that imply an obligation to help facilitate it?

A: There is little guidance on this issue. The first principal of the foundation for this report is to protect the community and then try to rehabilitate the offender. If courts are to impose abstinence requirements, considering the difficulty of behavior change, then it is reasonable to ask how they might help an offender attain that goal. DWI courts, where available, could help provide a solution. An interlock program that links treatment and BAC data can serve both of those interests (p 41-42).

Q: Is there any precedent for linking treatment and interlock program data? How can we make the best use of the breath test record (data log file) for both safety and rehabilitation of the offenders? Should the interlock breath test log file be used as one of several criteria – as a supplemental source of information to support the need for treatment/ counseling support?

A: Several States use interlock information; few integrate the interlock with treatment. West Virginia requires offenders in an interlock program also to enroll in an alcohol safety treatment program. Virginia's case managers have direct treatment links. They serve as a center point of action between the offenders, the courts, treatment, and the interlock provider (p. 42).

6. Key Differences in Court Programs and Motor Vehicle Authority Programs

Q: Administrative and judicial programs are different. Administrative programs can be managed more easily with a consistent set of rules, whereas court programs vary by court. On the other hand, court programs have considerably more leverage in helping offenders to change their behavior by having the ability to apply additional sanctions. How can each serve the community interests best?

A: Key differences and the reasons for them are described (p. 42).

Q: Evidence has suggested that there are pros and cons to both administrative and judicial interlock programs. Should we favor hybrid (administrative and court) programs to maximize the potential safety benefit of the interlock?

A: Yes, several States including New Mexico and Florida have hybrid programs (p.43-44). Hybrid programs can operate under the authority of the court, but they use the centralized management and monitoring of the licensing authority to manage vendor and offender compliance.

Q: If the interlock program fails to control the drinking-driving of an offender adequately, what alternative means of monitoring are available?

A: Depending on the type of program and whether there is an abstinence requirement imposed, other methods, such as alcohol monitoring bracelets and alcohol biomarkers, can serve this purpose (p 44-45).

7. Core Elements to Consider for Ignition Interlock Programs

Q: What is a reasonable set of core recommendations for all interlock programs, regardless of any regional or philosophical differences? What do they all need? What type of enabling legislation should be recommended?

A: There is no simple consensus answer to this question, the report lists dozens of recommendations and these are sorted into five broad categories: public understanding and deterrence; policy and management of the program; monitoring and reporting; issues for the judiciary, and other topics (p.46-49).

Q: Can New Mexico's hybrid judicial and administrative program serve as a model for other States? Where can its laws be found? What is it missing? Has there been an evaluation of New Mexico's interlock program?

A: New Mexico has enacted a set of laws that have led to a 50 percent installation rate among convicted DWI offenders and, in combination with other State initiatives, have contributed to significant statewide reductions in recidivism (p. 50).

8. Miscellaneous Other Topics

Q: What about rural programs? Should there be accommodations to the driving distances required for those who live a long way from a service center?

A: Described are methods employed by several interlock providers to address the needs of rural residents. No specific recommendation has been made. (p. 51; Marques, Tippetts, & Voas, 2003).

Q: Should there be emergency overrides?

A: An override capability has been provided in Quebec, Canada with evidence that offenders who used it had slightly higher recidivism rates. In Florida, driving after override causes lights to flash and the horn to blow (p. 51).

Q: Are there DWI offenders who should receive early release from the interlock obligation?

A: If this is done, the interlock BAC record should be supplemented with other measures, such as urine or blood alcohol biomarkers to assure drinking is under control (p. 52).

Q: Should motorcycles be fitted with interlocks?

A: No recommendation, but if used, retests should be taken only while the motorcycle is stationary (p.52).

Q: The NHTSA Model Specifications for Breath Alcohol Ignition Interlock Devices do not offer recommendations for interlock programs, only equipment operating within those programs (BAIIDS, 1972). The discussion of key features needed for interlock programs assume that equipment conforming to NHTSA Model Specifications is in service within the States.

A: States need to establish both equipment standards and program standards to maximize an interlock safety impact. This section closes with some discussion of topics that, while part of the Model Specifications, have implications for Program Standards (e.g., calibration intervals, retest refusals, retest failures). (p. 53-54).

Summary and Conclusion

This document represents the authors' interpretation of the evidence from sources including a compilation of other information concerning ignition interlocks, including the literature, ICADTS survey results and the discussions with leading practitioners, researchers and others, individually and during an expert panel meeting. All participants in the expert panel meeting received a copy of the first draft of the report and were given the opportunity to comment.

Conceivably, the best way to proceed regarding ignition interlocks is to impose on offenders a level of monitoring and restriction that matches the level of public risk that they represent. In the absence of any clear guidelines, States have developed a variety of approaches to the use of alcohol ignition interlocks. These efforts have yielded the evidence that today we must sift through to make recommendations about the most promising way to proceed with ignition interlock programs. The program structures that have been put in place reflect differing philosophies, none of which are all right or all wrong. While it is clear that interlocks reduce recidivism overall, few of the specific program models have been evaluated adequately. As a result, no single program is known to have satisfactorily addressed all the implementation and control problems.

A pragmatic view would favor reducing the risk of alcohol crashes above all other considerations. For DWI offenders, the evidence at this stage suggests we should install interlocks early, keep them installed until there is evidence of behavior change, perform active monitoring of both offender and vendor performance during the interlock program, and heavily ramp up consequences for noncompliance to ensure that driving while suspended is not a low-risk alternative to the interlock. Those offenders who have violated the terms of an interlock assignment on a license suspension/revocation for DWI should be subject to more restrictive behavior controls, such as monitoring bracelets. Offenders are likely to feel that, relative to wearing a monitoring bracelet on the ankle, the interlock on the vehicle will be a less expensive and more appealing alternative.

Background on Ignition Interlocks

Interlock description: The alcohol ignition interlock (sometimes referred to as a "BAIID," breath alcohol ignition interlock device) is a device attached to the ignition of a vehicle that requires the operator to provide a breath sample for analysis of alcohol level each time the engine is started. In most applications, the user is a convicted DWI offender who is required to undergo a period of interlock-controlled driving to be eligible for full license reinstatement, or in other applications, the offender can choose to shorten the period of full hard suspension with an interlock restricted license.

The interlocks have four basic elements: (1) a breath alcohol sensor in the vehicle (and a control unit under the hood) that records the driver's BAC and can be set to provide a warning if any alcohol is detected and, based on some criteria, such as the NHTSA Model Specifications, that recommends the vehicle not start if the BAC is .025 g/dL or higher; (2) a rolling retest system, which requires at least one retest after the vehicle is underway, but in most applications a retest is required every 20 to 30 minutes while driving (the purpose of the retest is to prevent a non-driver from starting the vehicle for a person who has been drinking and also to prevent drinking once the vehicle is underway); (3) a tamper-proof system for mounting the engine part of the unit, which is inspected every 30 to 60 days to preclude circumvention, along with a system to detect hot-wiring or other means that bypass the interlock; and (4) a data-recording system that logs the BAC results, tests compliance, and engine operation to determine whether the offender is actually using the vehicle as expected and not simply parking it while driving another vehicle.

History of interlock development: The first interlock was developed by Borg-Warner Corp. (now BorgWarner, Inc.), in 1969. After performance-based interlocks were tried and rejected in the 1970s, alcohol-sensing devices became the standard through the 1980s. They employed semiconductor (nonspecific) alcohol sensors. Semiconductor-type (Taguchi) interlocks were sturdy and got the field moving, but did not hold calibration very well, were sensitive to altitude variation and reacted positively to non-alcohol sources. Commercialization and more widespread adoption of the device was delayed pending improvement of systems for preventing circumvention. By the early 1990s, the industry began to produce "second generation" interlocks with reliable and accurate fuel cell sensors.

Interlock model specifications: In 1992, NHTSA issued "Model Specifications for Breath Alcohol Ignition Interlock Devices" (NHTSA, 1992), which recommended standards for sensitivity and reliability testing and provided for the incorporation of rolling retests and datarecording systems on ignition interlocks to make circumvention difficult. The improvements in this technology have left the use of a non-interlock vehicle as the only uncontrolled method for circumventing the interlock. The illicit driving of a noninterlocked vehicle, which is a drivingwhile-suspended (DWS) offense, remains an important limitation of the interlock technology. However, despite the opportunity to use another vehicle, there is substantial evidence that interlocks reduce recidivism while installed on vehicles.

Evidence for equipment effectiveness: There is no controversy in the field that interlocks, when used, are effective in reducing the recidivism of drivers convicted of driving while impaired (DWI). There are currently about 15 studies in the literature. Evidence from most demonstrates 35 to 75 percent effectiveness *while installed on the vehicle* (DeYoung, Tashima, & Maston, 2005; Coben & Larkin, 1999; Voas, Marques, Tippetts, & Beirness, 1999). A recent meta-analysis by Willis, Lybrand, and Bellamy (2004), performed under the Cochrane Collaboration rules for selecting studies for inclusion in a meta-analysis, found that, while installed, the interlock reduced the relative risk of DWI recidivism to .36 (a 64% reduction). Once the interlock is removed from the vehicle, the recidivism rate returns to the level of similar offenders who have not installed interlocks. The fact that when the interlock is on the offender's vehicle recidivism is reduced, compared to when it is not on the vehicle, demonstrates that it is an effective method for incapacitating the offender but that it has relatively little value in modifying long-term behavior. The fact that recidivism is not very different for the interlock and non-interlock groups after the interlock is removed is useful evidence that the groups under study probably do not differ very much in basic risk likelihood.

Limited program effectiveness: A major limitation on the safety impact of interlocks has been the weakness of interlock laws, the reticence of some judges to impose interlocks and the resistance of offenders to installing them. In addition, some localities lack interlock providers. As a result, even in States with full legislative support, a mere 10 to 20 percent of offenders eligible for interlock programs generally install the devices (Voas, Blackman, Tippetts, & Marques, 2002). Approximately 1.4 million DWI arrests are made each year (FBI, 2007). Only a portion of arrests result in convictions and, in most States, only some offenders are eligible for interlocks, Nonetheless, about 100,000 interlocks were in use in 2006; 133,000 in 2007, 145,000 in 2008, and 180,000 in 2009 (Roth, 2009). Among the problems that limit the number of interlocks in use are laws that allow an offender to refuse an interlock merely by stating that the offender agrees not to drive, or claiming that the offender does not own a vehicle. Evaluation of those claims in New Mexico, where interlocks are mandatory has determined that those who opt out of the interlock on those bases have higher rates of DWI recidivism than those who install interlocks (Marques et al., 2009). Other problems that minimize interlock use include State laws that require lengthy periods of "hard" suspension, judges' lack of confidence in the effectiveness of interlocks, and the concern of some courts that the offender cannot pay for the interlock. Convincing judges to use the interlock (even in States that have an indigent fund to offset costs) and to monitor and enforce the requirement has proven to be a significant barrier to greater penetration.

Administrative versus judicial programs: Interlock programs divide into those that are primarily administered by the courts and those that are managed by the State licensing authority. There are advantages and disadvantages to each type; the most fundamental difference is that State licensing authorities are more likely to order the use of interlocks than the courts but the courts that do order interlocks can more effectively enforce the ignition interlock requirement by assigning harsher sanctions if an offender refuses to comply. By contrast, administrative interlock programs managed by the State licensing authorities have only the power to withhold the driving privilege. Although the State administrative programs lack the enforcement authority of the courts, their great advantage is that a single authority manages and monitors the program. This allows for much more uniform application of the program.

As noted above, variation in interlock deployment among court-based programs can be traced to the extremely wide judicial discretion, even when underlying State laws may mandate use of the ignition interlock for DWI convictions. Judges and prosecutors who choose to use interlocks vary substantially in their monitoring and enforcement of the court order. So far, it appears that two of the most successful administrative programs can attract about 25 to 40 percent of offenders into the interlock program (e.g., Florida and Quebec), which is good, but not enough to yield substantial Statewide reductions in alcohol-related injury crashes. Yet, some State judicial programs like those in Texas and California that require the interlock for multiple offenders, have use rates that appear to be significantly lower than those of the higher use administrative program States. There has not yet been a statewide evaluation of use in Texas, but estimates based on FBI statistics suggest that only about 10 percent of offenders there receive interlocks. In California, DeYoung (2005) reported only about 2 to 5 percent of offenders receive interlocks through the court system, and independent estimates based on manufacturer census and FBI data (Roth, 2006) suggest the number in California is less than 3 percent. However, judicial programs can work very well. By virtue of a set of five mutually supporting laws passed over 7 years, the New Mexico statewide judicial interlock program is setting a new standard for installation rates. As of August 2008, New Mexico is estimated to have accomplished nearly a 50-percent installation rate (Marques, Voas, Roth, & Tippetts, 2009, in press). Notably, New Mexico has a program with both judicial (the mandatory laws) and administrative (the licensing act) components.

Untapped potential: Research evidence from Alberta, Quebec, Texas, and New Mexico, based on more than 50 million interlock breath tests, has firmly documented that the log of BAC tests contained in the interlock record is a potent predictor of future DWI recidivism once the interlock is removed from the vehicle and the driver has returned to fully reinstated licensure. Those who have the highest rates of elevated BAC tests are at substantially higher likelihood of recidivism, and those who have elevated BAC tests in the morning have the highest rates of recidivism (due to a prior night of high-BAC drinking). These findings were published in a series of research reports by investigators at PIRE (Marques, Voas, Tippetts, & Beirness, 1999; Marques, Tippetts, Voas, & Beirness, 2001; Marques, Tippetts, & Voas, 2003a; Marques, Voas, & Tippetts, 2003b). Beginning in 2006 and continuing now, a few State interlock programs began making systematic use of this information in the stored interlock event record as part of either sentencing extensions or rehabilitation programs.

Potential benefit to DWI offender rehabilitation: The interlock has an important benefit for the offender: Installation of the device allows DWI offenders to maintain their responsibilities (e.g., driving to work, taking children to school, running errands, etc.), while also serving as a constant reminder that their privilege to drive is contingent on their sobriety. Other methods for incapacitating the offender, such as jail and house arrest, involve a much greater intrusion on their lives and on their families. The record of drinking that the device logs, a median 7 to 8 breath tests a day, also has the potential of providing useful information to a qualified therapist. Having a clear record of locked out engine starts due to BAC can at least theoretically help therapists build dialogue with resistant offenders and help offenders to confront and control their drinking. Self-report evidence from those who do drive with an interlock suggests that the majority of offenders are supportive of the interlock and, sometimes grudgingly, do recognize that it has helped keep them out of trouble by serving as a reminder to not drink and drive (Marques, Voas, Roth, & Tippetts, 2009).

Methods

The purpose of this effort has been to identify those areas of interlock program design and management that maximize the potential of interlocks to improve road safety for America. To that end, a wide variety of information was collected about interlock policies, practices, and opinions.

The sources from which this information was compiled included published and unpublished literature, pre-conference meetings, conference discussions, survey information acquired under the auspices of interlock groups outside government, information acquired from key informants in both the public and private sectors, and finally an all-day panel session of experts convened for the purpose of having an open interactive discussion.

Prior to the one day expert panel session, all participants in that meeting were given a written summary of findings from all previous project efforts to document what is currently understood about interlock programs, including an extensive survey of interlock experts representing 20 States with active interlock programs.

The summary drew heavily from responses to survey questions compiled by the Interlock Working Group (IWG) of the International Council of Alcohol Drugs and Traffic Safety (ICADTS). The questions populating the survey came to light during a conference discussion session in October 2006 at the 7th Annual Ignition Interlock Symposium in Colorado. That session attempted to uncover a spectrum of attendee views on important problem areas in interlock programs.

The session drew approximately 100 attendees. Following the meeting, the IWG of ICADTS constructed a survey and distributed it broadly to States with active interlock programs.

This report reflects a convergence of information and informed opinions about ignition interlock programs gathered from all of these sources, culminating in the expert panel.

Review of the published literature revealed no studies that had systematically evaluated interlock program elements. Much of the actual research effort on interlocks over the past 20 years has been devoted to the demonstration of device and program efficacy and effectiveness, not the effectiveness of program features or State laws.

Preliminary Meeting of Industry, Research, and Victim Advocacy

Prior to accumulating evidence from these various sources, a meeting was held in May 2006 to assess preliminary views whether the private sector interlock companies and the safety community hold different views regarding key elements of interlock programs. Attendees at that meeting included representatives of two major interlock companies (Ian Marples of Alcohol Countermeasure Systems Corp. and Jim Ballard of Smart Start, Inc.), interlock researchers (Dick Roth of Impact DWI, Inc., in New Mexico, Doug Beirness of the Canadian Centre on Substance Abuse, Ottawa, and the two authors of this report, Bob Voas and Paul Marques of PIRE), and victim advocates

(Chuck Hurley of MADD USA and Andy Murie of MADD Canada). This meeting was in advance of the IIS meeting, where an afternoon open discussion session devoted to interlock program features was held. At the preliminary meeting, there was general agreement, and seven themes emerged as important topics for interlock programs:

- **Prompt Installation:** reduce the long "hard suspension" periods so that interlocks can be installed more promptly (soon after the arrest) and lower the likelihood that offenders become accustomed to driving while suspended;
- **Develop Standardized Reporting:** encourage vendors to agree on standardized reporting criteria for both court and administrative programs;
- **Compliance/Criterion Based Removal:** require a period of "clean time" (no elevated BAC tests) before interlock removal and reinstatement;
- **Performance Monitoring and Interlock Extensions:** require adequate program monitoring of offender performance so there can be a lawful basis for an extension on the interlock program if there is continuing evidence of elevated BAC tests in the months before full reinstatement is scheduled;
- **Linkage To Treatment:** build better links with rehabilitation programs so therapists can use the record of breath tests and possibly engage medical review boards to assess driver fitness and help alcohol dependent offenders;
- **Programs Should Emphasize That the Priority Is to Prevent Impaired Driving:** build interlock programs that emphasize the separation of drinking and driving but do not attempt to position the interlock as a means to assure abstinence, which is a different problem (later it was learned in the expert panel that some, particularly those in the judiciary, insist that there be no drinking, not simply a separation of drinking and driving); and
- **Minimum Required Interlock Period:** require interlocks for at least one year for all offenders (disputed by some).

The preliminary views of this small group suggested that it will be possible to find accord among different interest groups. Disagreements were minor at this preliminary meeting, but certain key groups, such as judges and prosecutors, were not represented. Other viewpoints surfaced later.

It was also emphasized by the interlock companies that their experience has shown that if important safety features are not required by the State or the court, then vendors can (and some do) appeal directly to offenders (their prospective customers) and offer interlocks that may be easier to circumvent.

The Information-Gathering Process

After the preliminary meeting, during the IIS commentary about problem areas were identified in an hour-long open discussion session. These issues were compiled into a survey. The survey, developed under the auspices of the IWG, was not a NHTSA activity, but it was concurrent and thematically similar to NHTSA's effort to document ignition interlock implementation problem areas and to identify key elements needed in interlock programs. The results are included here. The survey questions are contained in Appendix A.

The IWG survey participants were comprised of practitioners and evaluators from 20 States, 2 Canadian Provinces and 2 countries outside of North America. Domestically, the sampling plan for acquiring input was tilted intentionally toward individuals in States with substantial interlock experience. Respondents also included interlock experts identified by the Governors Highway Safety Representatives. The targeting of those States having experienced people was based on a 2006 survey of all interlock providers (now annually updated), compiled by Impact DWI's Roth (Roth, 2009). His State-by-State estimate of interlocks in service was based on direct reports from device manufacturers. We used his estimates to rank States into those with considerable interlock experience (more than 2,000 units in service) and those with relatively less experience. Among the States using the most interlocks, at least one key informant commented from 13 of the 15 States. Tables 1 and 2 show check marks by the States where someone provided input. Table 1 includes the States with more than 2,000 interlocks in service as of June 2006. Table 2 represents those States with fewer than 2,000 interlocks where someone also provided commentary.

Information compiled from these sources was summarized and provided as pre-read content for members of the expert panel. The Agenda for the expert panel Meeting provided an overview of topic areas mentioned by survey respondents. While not all the pre-meeting discussion topics were addressed during the one-day panel, many of the key topics did receive attention.

Table 1. States with more than 2,000 interlocks in service as of August 2006. A check denotes having received input from at least one person

State	Total	State	Total	State	Total	State	Total
TX	✓	FL	✓	MI	✓	IL	✓
WA	✓	NM	✓	AZ	✓	PA	✓
NC	✓	IA		VA	✓	OH	
CA	✓	MD	✓	CO	✓		

Table 2. States with at least one but fewer than 2,000 interlocks in service as of June 2006. A check denotes having received input from at least one person

State	Total	State	Total	State	Total	State	Total	State	Total	State	Total
MO		WI	✓	NE		DE	✓	CT		ME	
OK	✓	LA		NV		SD		MN		NH	✓
GA		NY	✓	NJ		KY		SC		VT	
AR		WV	✓	TN		MT		HI			
OR		KS		MA		AK		AL			
UT		ID	✓	IN		MS		WY			

The Expert Panel

The expert panel, served as the final step in providing information on interlocks, and it set the stage for producing a summary of commentary and dialog on programs and procedures.

The one-day expert panel session convened on October 4, 2007, and was comprised of 28 people selected for the breadth of their interlock expertise from around North America. The views and expertise of the panel participants represented a spectrum of knowledge about the use of ignition interlock devices in the prevention and adjudication of DWI. Panelists included judges, prosecutors, defense attorneys, manufacturers, treatment professionals, State program managers, probation officers, interlock researchers, NHTSA officials, and the victim community, which was represented by MADD USA (at the table) and MADD Canada (in written commentary). Members of this panel are shown in Appendix B.

From 8 a.m. to 4 p.m., an engaged discussion among panelists explored ways in which breath alcohol ignition interlock programs can help the United States achieve some of its road safety goals and how to resolve current procedural problems that have been identified. Not all of the topics identified in this report were fully covered in the expert panel session, but many important issues were examined thoroughly.

The views expressed in this document form the basis for a wider conversation about what elements might one day be included in a "best practices" approach to interlock programs. However, considerably more outcome information will be needed before best practices can be understood on the basis of evidence.

The organization of the pre-meeting reading materials and the expert panel discussion are shown below, organized by their common themes. Specific topical issues are discussed in more detail further along in this report.

A Foundation for Interlock Programs

The following foundation had wide support among members of the expert panel. As an order of priority, it was agreed generally that interlocks should:

- Protect the community as a top priority,
- Help remediate problem drinkers to the extent possible, and
- Use the interlock to whatever extent possible for general deterrence.

Within the spirit of this foundation, basic principles and key features of ignition interlock programs were identified and are discussed below. While not identical, some of the organizing themes are similar to those discussed in the small group meeting in May 2006. States and communities attempting to set up ignition interlock programs likely will benefit from this information. The following section serves as an overview of topics that are developed in more detail further along in this report. Wherever possible, a recommendation is provided at the end of each topic. When no clear recommendation is possible, contrasting views are summarized.

Overview of Key Features in Interlock Programs

1. Installation and Program Enrollment Issues

Nearly all programs have low enrollment/installation/penetration relative to the annual number of DWI arrests and convictions. Knowing that the average reduction in DWI recidivism is reduced by about 65 percent while interlocks are installed, how can we improve interlock use/enrollment? How long should someone be on a program? How soon after arrest should an interlock be available?

- Should first-time DWI offenders be included in interlock programs?
- Should reinstatement of driving privileges after a DWI conviction require a period of interlock controlled driving?
- Should the interlock requirement be added to those with hardship or limited licenses? Similarly, should interlock drivers be able to drive without limits or, in some cases, be issued a limited or hardship license?
- How long should suspension/revocation periods extend before interlock eligibility? That is, should there be support for early interlock installation following arrest or conviction? Or should traditional lengthy suspension periods prior to interlock be encouraged?
- What is a reasonable duration for interlock programs?

2. Interlock Program Ramp-Up and Expansion

- What concrete advice can be offered to States ready to start up or make major expansions? How can they learn from the experiences of others?
- What should an interlock program cost offenders?
- How should programs accommodate low income or indigent offenders?
- What circumvention protections should new programs be attuned to?
- How should interlock providers (vendors) be managed? Should there be a controlled number of vendors or an open competition in each State?

3. Standardization of Reporting and Information Flow

- Communication and information flow is organized haphazardly in many State programs. How can we improve information moving from: private industry to administrators, administrators to courts/ probation, courts to offenders, all to each other?
- What type of reporting formats from service providers to monitoring authority should be recommended or required?
- Should there be a minimal vehicle use requirement to guard against the offender parking the vehicle and waiting out a required interlock period?

4. Program Compliance, Noncompliance, and Interlock Removal

- Should there be different consequences for different types of noncompliance? Procedural violations and circumvention attempts differ from BAC levels recorded as locked out starts in the data log file. Should States regard these differently?
- How should States address issues of BAC lockouts?
- Should there be different performance expectations placed on the offender as a function of time on program? Should the monitoring authority's definition of "compliance" become stricter after months of practice using an interlock?
- Should there be extensions on interlock programs for some offenders with repeated lockout BAC tests? What should trigger an extension in the interlock program?
- Now that BAC monitoring of DWI offenders is possible via the interlock breath test record, should programs require a demonstration that a driver is no longer logging alcohol lockouts before ending the interlock requirement and dispensing an unrestricted driver's license?
- How can we reconcile the core design of interlocks (to prevent impaired driving) with the desire of some court programs to use interlocks as an abstinence monitoring tool? What are the implications of these different philosophies for dealing with BAC lockouts or program extensions?
- Is the development of standards for two types of programs the way to resolve this abstinence now versus graded attainment of drinking control?

5. Linkage to Treatment

- The evidence shows that many treatment interventions linked to DWI sanctions have only a modest impact and are not systematically structured, monitored, evaluated, or applied. Does the interlock, with its data record of BAC tests, hold promise for improving the effectiveness of DWI treatment interventions? Or should these remain separate parts of the remediation process?
- If the government demands abstinence, does that imply an obligation to help facilitate it?
- Is there any precedent for linking treatment and interlock program data? How can we make the best use of the breath test record (the data log file) for both safety and rehabilitation of the offenders? Should the interlock breath test log file be used as one of several criteria – as a supplemental source of information to support the need for treatment/counseling support?

6. Key Differences in Court Programs and Motor Vehicle Authority Programs

- Administrative and judicial programs are different. Administrative programs can be managed more easily with a consistent set of rules whereas court programs vary by court. On the other hand, court programs have considerably more leverage in helping to goad offenders to change their behavior by having the ability to apply additional sanctions. How can each serve the community interests best?
- Evidence has suggested that there are pros and cons to both administrative and judicial interlock programs. Should we favor hybrid (administrative and court) programs to maximize the potential safety benefit of the interlock?
- If the interlock program fails to adequately control the drinking-driving of an offender, what alternative means of monitoring are available?

7. Core Elements to Consider for Ignition Interlock Programs

- What is a reasonable set of core recommendations for all interlock programs, regardless of any regional or philosophical differences? What do they all need? What type of enabling legislation should be recommended?

- Can New Mexico's hybrid judicial and administrative program serve as a model for other States? Where can its laws be found? What is it missing? Has there been an evaluation of New Mexico's interlock program?

8. Miscellaneous Other Topics

- What about rural programs? Should there be accommodations to the long driving distances required for those who live a long way from a service center?
- Should there be emergency overrides?
- Are there DWI offenders who should receive early release from the interlock obligation?
- Should motorcycles be fitted with interlocks?
- Device certification issues are not interlock program issues but found in the NHTSA Model Specifications for Breath Alcohol Ignition Interlock Devices. Key elements for a program assumes adequate equipment is required and in service within the States.

Because there is no formal research available on many of these topics, the experiences of program managers, researchers, judges, government authorities, and vendors is our best guide to reasonable answers. Opinion or anecdotes can often represent deep wells of experience in a wide variety of program types. Accordingly, the discussion topics selected for the expert panel came from the informed opinions of many and were extracted from many sources. The expert panel provided an important airing of these opinions and the following sections are an attempt to draw conclusions and recommendations from those discussions.

KEY FEATURES OF INTERLOCK PROGRAMS

Introduction

The most general statement about current interlock programs is that in the absence of any clear model or best practice, a wide variety of approaches have been implemented at the State level, including many very creative innovations. There has been ample evaluation of overall interlock effectiveness in many

States. However, very few individual interlock program features have been evaluated in any formal way.

As a general characterization, it appears that programs sort along a continuum, with some maintaining a primarily pragmatic public safety focus (if the interlock controls impaired driving, that is sufficient), some more strongly emphasize a desire for rehabilitation by promoting treatment, and some have a punitive focus that seeks to goad behavior change (the interlock is a privilege, like the driver license, and it will be withdrawn for bad behavior). Sometimes, variations on these themes all exist within the same State. But regardless of the orientation, there are many key elements that all programs must grapple with in the process of making their programs work well.

During the expert panel meeting, many convergent themes were found on which experts generally agreed. This document will begin by addressing the many points of agreement. There was one particular theme that revealed conflicting opinions. That was the question of whether interlock program breath test data should be used to document adherence to a requirement of alcohol abstinence by program participants (often ordered by the courts). There were strong arguments on both sides of that view and these views are summarized in the section on interlock extensions. Differences in this view can be a central determinant of how a program is structured—that is, the nature of the program features selected may vary depending on the importance of abstinence as a goal versus preventing impaired driving as a goal. This difference is introduced here in a general way so readers are primed to be attentive to these different approaches as program features are discussed. Should positive locked out BAC tests be seen as violations, as evidence that the interlock is working as intended, or both?

In most States, the BAC lockout points differ only slightly by program and often reflect the 1992 NHTSA Model Specifications' recommended lockout level of .025 g/dL. Nonetheless, the meaning and consequences of elevated BAC tests can be vastly different by jurisdiction.

The views about locked out BAC tests ranged widely among expert panelists. One view was that a failed start test due to BAC requires no further consequence because a blocked start is evidence that the interlock is working and an episode of impaired driving was prevented. Alternatively, some programs regard one or two elevated BAC tests as clear violations, even though the vehicle would not start. In such programs, lockout events may lead to serious restrictions on driving, licensing and program continuation. So, the question becomes, should the interlock support an abstinence requirement or is the interlock program sufficient to protect the public from exposure to alcohol risk of these DWI offenders, since it locks out alcohol positive drivers? And if the interlock should be directed toward monitoring abstinence, does that imply that there should be a more concerted effort to help support offender behavior change via treatment services? Alcohol dependency is not an easy problem to solve. Is there a middle ground? Should a limited number and/or certain level of BAC positive tests during a "learning" period of time be expected initially while new behavior is acquired, following which more stringent requirements are imposed as interlock use time progresses? Because the disagreement on this topic is important, it is addressed in detail in this report in Section 4 under the topic: ***Philosophical Differences Regarding Elevated Interlock Breath Tests***.

Because of these philosophical differences about what exactly should be accomplished with an interlock program, it was concluded that any national interlock program guidelines will have to be attentive to these different views about the meaning of elevated BAC tests. Is the interlock a shield for the public, a punishment for the offender, or something in between? This seemed to be such a central issue that it was the first item of discussion at the expert panel session. But for the purposes of this report, it is discussed after the more basic and numerous points of general agreement are described. One conclusion on this issue that held sway is that the legislation that helps the licensing authority and courts work together in a hybrid fashion (as has been done in Florida and New Mexico) will be needed to build maximally effective programs.

The following sections provide discussions about the key elements and features of interlock programs. Under each general grouping of interlock program principles, elemental topics are described briefly based on published evidence where possible, or through opinions gathered from key informants and presented to the expert panel members. There was not time to address all of the principles, elements and features during the expert panel meeting. Some of the recommendations reflects the views of key informants who provided input prior to the expert panel meeting.

Before detailing issues and recommendations about ignition interlock programs, it is important to clarify the dividing line between interlock device certification testing, and interlock program elements. The latter is the topic of this report; the former is embodied in the NHTSA Model Specifications for Breath Alcohol Ignition Interlock Devices (1992). The NHTSA Model Specifications concern device accuracy, precision, temperature ranges, vibration, voltage, circumvention detection protocols, data storage, retrieval, and related issues--that is, the basic adequacy of the equipment. The Model

Specifications are NHTSA's recommendation to the States for how to evaluate several different areas of device adequacy. The Federal Government does not yet maintain a "conforming products list" of interlock equipment, so today it is still up to the States to decide which devices they find adequate based on their own certification standards. States can adopt any or all of the NHTSA recommendations. The interlock program features that we review here are about how those devices should be used in the interest of safety. Interlock programs begin with the assumption that the basic equipment is reliable and that it meets the minimum State standards. Accordingly, this document does not discuss technical standards, circumvention protocols (other than that they always should be used), threshold BAC for lockout, and other concerns of the Model Specifications. Commentary on interlock program features were also provided by people from three other countries and a brief summary of features in Western Australia, Sweden, and Canada can be found in Appendix C.

The recommendations that follow for the key elements and features of interlock programs represent the authors' interpretation of the disparate evidence, and reflects input from members of the expert panel and other key informants.

1. Installation and Program Enrollment Issues

- **First Offenders and Multiple Offenders**

  Since half to two-thirds of all DWI offenders are first-time offenders, if interlock programs are exclusively restricted to multiple offenders (which was the protocol adopted by the earliest interlock programs), they will not make a full contribution to the improvement of alcohol safety on the roadways. Evidence from evaluation studies has now clearly shown that first-time offenders who drive with interlocks attain recidivism reduction on par with multiple offenders—about 65 percent reduction while the interlocks are installed (Roth, Voas, & Marques, 2007b; Willis et al., 2004; Voas et al., 1999). Estimates of impaired driving of most first offenders find they have operated vehicles while impaired many times prior to their first conviction. The idea of extending interlock programs to firsttime offenders was widely embraced by the expert panel participants.

  Some States prefer to distinguish two types of first offenders: aggravated and non-aggravated, with the dividing line set at an arrest BAC of about .15 to .17 g/dL. This is a defensible distinction that often makes first offender legislation more acceptable to legislators. A small but growing number of States today require interlocks for all DWI offenders and do not maintain a distinction based on arrest BAC level.

- **Recommendation: First Offender Interlock Programs**
  Interlocks should be required for all DWI offenders. If interlocks are impractical for some offenders, alternative means of alcohol monitoring should be offered that impose an equivalent cost burden on the offender. There should be neither a lower nor a higher cost for those offenders who avoid an interlock.

- **The Path to an Unrestricted License Goes Through the Interlock Program**
  Several States now have established a requirement that offenders must participate in the interlock program before full reinstatement of their license is permitted. The importance of this requirement is that it means offenders cannot wait out the suspension or revocation period, and if they are to ever have their license reinstated, they must have a period of interlock-controlled driving. The risk of such policies is that the regulation may encourage people to leave the licensing control system altogether. Often, high-risk drivers will transfer vehicle ownership to other family members and claim no intention to drive, in attempt to avoid installing an interlock. We do not yet know how States with mandatory administrative interlock laws will deal with recalcitrant DWI offenders. However, we do need to explore methods for identifying the individuals who pose the greatest risk to the public. Interlocks as a condition of reinstatement may help sort this out, and mandatory court programs could force an offender to choose between alternative alcohol monitoring or control technologies that are available to the offender (e.g., house arrest; Secure Continuous Remote Alcohol Monitor [SCRAM]—a device that continuously detects the release of alcohol gas from the skin's surface; Sobrietor; InHom; products that require the offender to provide regular breath samples at home).

  - **Recommendation: Interlocks Mandatory for Re-licensing**
    Interlocks (or some form of alternative alcohol monitoring) should be required for all DWI offenders. Since the licensing authority may not be able to require the use of non-driving-related alcohol monitoring devices, the courts would have to insist on the alternative monitoring requirement through some hybrid or shared responsibility between these divisions of government. It would

seem that any program requiring an interlock as a path to reinstatement will need a parallel increase in the enforcement of licensing laws to counteract the possibility that a mandatory interlock requirement will encourage more unlicensed driving.

- **Interlock License: Restricted Driving or Unlimited Driving?**

  The availability of restricted "vocational" licenses, which allow an offender to drive to and from work, may create a disincentive for the offender to install an interlock. Additionally, "hardship" licenses are more difficult for the police to enforce than full suspension. No matter what the time of day, offenders might claim that they are on their way to work, or on some special trip related to their job. There is evidence that DWI offenders with vocational licenses are less likely to reinstate their full licenses than offenders who do not receive such licenses (McKnight & Voas, 1991). One Expert Panelexpert panelist suggested that States with vocational license laws that do not now require an interlock as a prerequisite to a hardship license should consider adding the interlock requirement to their law.

  Most interlock programs allow offenders to drive anywhere anytime, but there are some State interlock programs that allow the interlock only with an occupational license – where the offender can go only to and from work. This is the case with first offenders in Wisconsin. The Michigan program restricts driving only for travel to work, alcohol treatment, court-ordered probation, community service, school and medical treatment. In Florida, first offenders are not restricted, but multiple offenders are restricted to education or employment-related driving, and the court can impose any reasonable restriction. A panel member noted that, in Westchester, New York, an interlock license issued by the Motor Vehicle Authority can be restricted or unrestricted. Even if unrestricted, the probation officer can determine when and where the offender can drive.

  - **Recommendation: Use of a Limited/Restricted Interlock Licenses**

    If restrictions on the interlock license are imposed (e.g., driving only to and from work), this may be counterproductive. But it is also an area where public opinion considerations may warrant using an initial restriction that could later be lifted for good behavior (e.g., evidence of regular vehicle use, but no BAC lockouts might be a criterion for an unlimited interlock license). On the other hand, the larger problem is enrollment, and initial limits on how an offender uses an interlock-equipped vehicle might further dissuade enrollment in the interlock programs. While some offenders may warrant a limited interlock license for a variable period, States that have achieved excellent DWI recidivism reductions with interlock programs have not used limited interlock licenses.

- **Early Entry Into Interlock Programs**

  Related to the issue of interlock requirement for reinstatement is the promptness of interlock installation and whether lengthy suspension periods should precede the interlock. Many of the interview-and-survey respondents agreed that if *early* reinstatement with the interlock could reduce the rate of driving while suspended (DWS) (presumably by limiting the opportunity to discover how easy it is to drive unlicensed and undetected), then it would be a win-win outcome for both the offender and public safety (not to mention the interlock companies). New Mexico did away with most of the required hard suspension period and made an interlock license available to any convicted offender (with a few minor exceptions). This approach can be controversial, however, because of evidence that suspended drivers may drive less and drive more carefully than reinstated drivers. On the other hand, the interlock often is not a favored option for offenders and, in New Mexico, like many other States, offenders can wait out the required interlock period if they successfully argue that they do not own a motor vehicle. Therefore, evidence about the comparative benefit of the hard suspension requirement versus interlock is needed. License suspension was a "hard won" victory of the safety community and, at the time suspension was strongly advocated, interlocks were not part of the discussion. In light of interlocks, is it necessary to have hard suspension before entering an interlock program? Or does suspension still serve a useful safety function to restrain careless and impaired driving?

  The IWG survey findings showed that some States cite the barrier created by Federal legislation (the Transportation Equity Act for the 21st Century, or TEA-21) as the reason they still require 6 or more months of hard suspension, but this would be largely resolved now with the June 2008 technical corrections to the Safe, Accountable, Flexible, Efficient Transportation Equity Act: A Legacy for Users (SAFETEA-LU), which superseded TEA-21, that now allows for earlier installation.

  - **Recommendation: Early Entry into Interlock Programs**
    Studies have shown that the first 6 months following a DWI conviction hold the highest likelihood of recidivism. DWI offenders should be controlled by an interlock during that period. Expert panel members were generally in favor of early entry into interlock programs. Most realized, however, that we need controlled evaluation studies to determine how much, if any, hard suspension (no driving at all) adds to public safety and whether any of that safety benefit is forfeited with early interlocks.
- **Program Duration**
  The primary question here is how much time should be required on the interlock. There is no research evidence that bears on this question at this time, and practices differ by jurisdiction. Nonetheless, practices are not widely different among the States.
  Not only is there no hard evidence to suggest the best lengths of interlock duration. As a scientific question, we still do not know how long administrative license revocation (ALR) should continue if it is to be maximally effective. ALR has been used widely for more years than interlocks. In the absence of any clear models or guidance, States developing or hoping to improve their programs typically follow the lead of other States. The general pattern is that more time is given to higher risk (e.g., arrest BAC $\geq .15$ g/dL) or repeat offender status. In sampling opinion, several key informants noted that anything less than 6 months for the lower risk DWI offender (first offender with arrest BAC $< .15$ g/dL) is unsupportable, whereas others believed that at least one year is appropriate for this category of offender. For other offenders, such as second and third offenders, 2 and 3 years on the interlock, respectively, was suggested. For four or more offenses, New Mexico (arguably now having the most successful program with about half of its convicted offenders installing interlocks) imposes a lifetime interlock with a 5-year review. At the panel session, it was mentioned, and no disagreements registered, that the worst possible outcome is to engage in serial exercises of catch and release, such that offenders are cycled through a repeat pattern of offense, sanction, release, and reissuance of their license, only to repeat the cycle over again. Many jurisdictions have offenders with 10 or more prior DWI offenses on their records; some with well over 20. As Chuck Hurley, CEO of MADD, noted at its First Technology Summit in Albuquerque in 2006, shortly after launching MADD's Campaign to

Eliminate Drunk Driving, residents of many States find it alarming that they share the road with thousands of offenders who have five or more prior DWI offenses on their record. Based on this type of public concern, now including evidence that 84 percent of the public favor interlocks for DWI offenders (McCartt et al., 2009), there is a broad support for the use of interlocks as a tool to enhance public safety, at least when directed toward DWI offenders.

Along the lines of engaging community support, members of the expert panel suggested that there be at least some nod to the public sense of proportionality, such that those with more priors or higher arrest BACs should be sanctioned more severely. From a safety viewpoint, it is reasonable to want the interlocks installed soon after conviction, and some experts argued that hard suspension periods before interlock eligibility should be much shorter (e.g., 30 to 60 days) than in the past (6 to 36 months). However, others still maintained that higher risk multiple and other higher risk offenders should receive lengthier hard suspensions as well as lengthier periods of driving without lockout BAC events once in an interlock program.

Regarding the latter, some States have written provisions for extending the duration of the required interlock installation period for drivers who have procedural violations or who continue to blow elevated BAC tests throughout the interlock period. At the session, there was panelist commentary from States that do not have the legislative authority to extend the interlock period but like the idea, despite feeling concerned that it may impose another large management burden on the licensing authority.

- **Recommendation: Program Duration**

  The expert panel did not explicitly discuss interlock duration other than to endorse the proportionality principle, such that longer interlock requirements should apply to those with aggravated or more prior DWI convictions. The New Mexico laws for installation duration are simple and straightforward: one year for first offenders, two for second offenders, three for third offenders and lifetime interlock with 5-year review for offenders with four or more prior DWIs. The Florida law stipulates 6 months for high-BAC first offenders, one year for second offenders unless arrest BAC =.20 or greater, which triggers a two-year interlock requirement. New Mexico's stipulated interlock periods are on the longer end of the continuum among the States, but there was no suggestion at the Panel meeting that these durations were either inappropriate or unsupportable; quite the contrary, many favored them. It was also suggested by expert panel members that those who refuse BAC tests should be required to be subject to longer required interlock time.

2. Ignition Interlock Program Ramp Up and Expansion

A very practical problem that was considered by the expert panel addressed how to best assist States that are about to undertake a large step toward system-wide expansion of their interlock programs. The panel provided helpful insight. For example, several States are initiating statewide mandatory programs and are expecting rapid growth from small or littleused interlock programs, and some (e.g., Illinois) were preparing for a program to increase as much as tenfold (from a thousand to potentially tens of thousands annually). The panelists discussed the pros and cons of a phase-in versus a rapid expansion.

- **Considerations for Developing or Expanding an Interlock Program**

  The general theme in the discussions took on a tone of preparing the public for the program, preparing various divisions of Government for the program, arranging for the technical resources that will be needed, embracing natural adversaries as part of the engagement process, working with the private companies that eventually will provide the services, deciding on compliance and noncompliance criteria, and explicitly spelling out what those should be. It was suggested that policy decisions drafted at the beginning of the process can head off problems later on. Not everyone agreed on all of the suggestions that were raised, but none elicited vocal opposition either. The following recommendations were voiced and are worthy of consideration.
- **Recommendations: Program Ramp Up**

1. It would be helpful to have a NHTSA-endorsed outreach or technical assistance team comprised of a small group with expertise on various pragmatic problems. Some of this expertise can be uniquely provided by manufacturers, but there should be others involved who have no business interests at stake.
2. There should be a public information campaign launched along with the interlock program that broadly educates the public and, in so doing, also improves general deterrence. The message

should inform listeners that interlock programs can allow DWI offenders to drive, but only when there is no alcohol involved. Interlocks should not be perceived as a program that coddles offenders.

3. Infrastructure for service delivery can be provided by vendors, but the State must clearly define the requirements for vendors who provide service in the State. (See later discussion on setting a common format for reports.)
4. The type of State-level response will differ, depending on whether it is an administrative or a court program. For this reason, the courts and the State must work together to find common ground. All Canadian programs are administrative; in the United States, programs are either judicial, administrative or both.
5. In New Mexico, initially the program was solely judicial and the statewide implementation group was small, but over time, it expanded to include various State agencies, including district attorney's offices, representatives from the Departments of Health and Public Safety, the attorney general, and others. Having prosecutors as part of the group brought a new perspective to the challenges faced by the State in interlock implementation. Currently, prosecutors arrange trainings for other prosecutors, police officers, DWI county coordinators, probation officers and other State officials involved in the ignition interlock program. Educational programs are organized throughout the State to inform State agencies, the courts, and the public on the intricacies of the interlock system and the challenges to reducing DWI prevalence in New Mexico.
6. Florida established a similar implementation work group. This group served as a DWI technical advisory committee, and was comprised of law enforcement, judges, prosecutors, and State licensing administrators. Note that in Florida, there are consequences for BAC test failures, so it requires a lot of monitoring.
7. Florida representatives had several specific suggestions based on their experience. These included the following:
    a. There must be a capability to deal with vendor issues and medical issues (e.g., having a pulmonologist or other physician available to review requests from offenders for

exceptions from the interlock requirements). Note: Maryland has a Medical Review Board for issues of this kind.

b. The administrative program will work best if there is a good working relationship with judiciary.
c. There needs to be a State monitoring board that visits providers (presumably involving unannounced visits and sanctioning or remediation protocols imposed for noncompliance, that are jointly developed by the State and private vendors).
d. There must be staff resources at the administrative offices to conduct monitoring.
e. There should be inclusion of educational programs for lower risk offenders and referral and treatment programs for higher risk offenders.

More generally, beyond the experiences of Florida and New Mexico, many other suggestions and recommendations were made by expert panel participants.

8. Make an effort to find key stakeholders in each community (community broadly defined) and engage them in the development process.
9. Engage the alcohol/drug treatment community from the beginning, so they can come to understand the interlock program and decide how to best use the interlock breath-test record in their work. No treatment requirement should be reduced or waived in exchange for participation in an interlock program. Rather, treatment and interlock programs are a natural fit and should function jointly.
10. During the planning process, include potential opponents of the interlock or DWI interventions. The inclusion of potential opponents is an important part of attaining objections and should be considered just one part of a broad effort to engage the general public.
11. Smooth the implementation by deciding in advance what contents are desired in a report and then ensuring that monitoring staff are completely familiar with monthly report formats (e.g., how to read a report). Reporting formats are discussed in the next section of this report.
12. Quebec, Canada, had a large ramp-up in installation rates at the start of its 1997 program. It set up objective compliance criteria.

Then, service providers/vendors devised a red-flag function that brought to the attention of the monitoring authority any offenders who were having high rates of lockouts or procedural violations. In Quebec, the manufacturer (as opposed to its agent providers of local service) retained responsibility for management and reporting to the provincial authority.

13. A survey could be conducted of resources within a State (e.g., What exists? What should be built?). National level resources could be helpful in many ways; particularly, by brokering a technology-sharing function.
14. It was noted that interlock legislation is complex, and it is important to invest effort at the beginning, both to obtain buy-in and to smooth implementation.
15. Since there are different devices, different providers/vendors and different roles for various participants in the interlock program, the State should require training for anyone who is tasked with monitoring vendor performance or reviewing reports.
16. States must consider whether they want to have a sole provider or two or more vendors. Free market considerations favor multiple providers; management burden may favor fewer, so they can be organized more easily. There is no single answer; there are benefits and liabilities to all arrangements. Florida licenses only two providers, one for the north and one for the south; New Mexico uses six different providers.
17. In rural areas, it may be too costly for interlock companies to open and staff service centers, and a common solution to this is for the interlock companies to contract with other automotive service providers (e.g., auto sound systems, auto electrical repairs or auto glass) who can be trained as interlock service technicians. Malouin and Brosseau (2005) reported on the benefits and potential conflicts of this arrangement for center employees who must juggle roles as customer-care oriented business people and safety technicians representing Government interests.
18. Vendor performance standards for equipment checks should be established as should standards for the supervision of providers who send reports. To minimize the burden of review, reports should be based on exception (e.g., failed BAC tests that warrant attention of the monitoring authority should be flagged rather than

the authority having the burden of searching the entire record). The exception criteria should be fully specified in advance.

19. Outside experts could help the start-up State to:
    a. predict staffing needs;
    b. help define vendor expectations;
    c. consider indigent funds; and
    d. define reporting protocols and responsibilities, minimal data needs, etc.
20. A process should be developed for any States that will be adopting new laws, as all will have a need for pragmatic advice.
21. All offenders who are required to drive exclusively with an interlock should have a bold “interlock” restriction placed on their driver license for the benefit of both in-State and out-of-State law enforcement officers.
22. Finally, the State should engage all relevant parties so that technical assistance is not rejected a priori. Various interest groups within a State need to understand that interlocks require some specialized knowledge.

These suggestions formed the content of a discussion about how government or other organizations could help States plan for a large expansion of their interlock programs. States also will need to decide about other pragmatic topics.

- **What Should Interlock Programs Cost?**

  Cost is a key consideration. In most States, offender costs are in the same range, \$65 to \$90 a month, not including installation fees, which reportedly can run from approximately \$100 to \$250. With installation insurance, plus basic fees, a typical cost cited was \$1,000 to \$1,500 per year (at the upper end). Including installation, this equates to approximately \$70 to \$125 per month. In Arizona, offenders pay for interlock costs and the State uses fees from aggravated DWI and extreme DWI to pay for Department of Motor Vehicle (DMV) staff costs. New Mexico has a statewide indigent fund that can be used by local court systems to offset offender costs, but has no agreed-upon standards for its use. In Texas, the monitoring fee is \$10 per month.

  1. It was noted that each DWI in New Mexico is estimated to cost the State \$50,000. An effective interlock program can facilitate cost offset. Roth et al., (2007) estimated a \$5-to-\$1 benefit-to-cost

ratio. The benefit accrues to the State while the cost goes to the offender.

2. Insurance is a significant cost item for DWI offenders. It was suggested that the reason Quebec had such a brisk enrollment in its interlock program after start up is the provincial government subsidizes of the cost of insurance. Is there a way to engage the insurance companies in the United States to this end?
3. Monthly interlock lease fees vary by program, but are usually in the range of \$60–\$90, unless there is some sort of cost offset for indigent offenders.
4. A few panelists suggested that the liquor excise tax should be increased or diverted to be used to offset the costs of monitoring interlock programs.

- **Recommendation: Interlock Program Cost**
  The interlock cost—approximately equivalent to 1 or 2 drinks per day—is much less than the cost of alcohol monitoring bracelets which at the time of this writing cost about \$12 to \$15 per day. The public safety benefit of having substantially more funds available to help defray costs to low income offenders has not been studied, but this would be a worthwhile topic for investigation. Two estimates (Roth et al., 2007b; Miller & Levy, 2000) of interlock program benefit/cost ratio have suggested that there is a \$4 to \$7 benefit to the State for each dollar the programs cost offenders. Some State investments in program monitoring may be warranted, since monitoring and enforcement can be key to program compliance. Arguably, States could reduce costs by supporting these programs.

- **Should There Be Cost Offset or Reduced Fees for Indigent Offenders?**
  Financial hardship is cited frequently by DWI offenders as a reason for avoiding an interlock when the opportunity is presented. It seems important to provide some kind of cost offset fund for true indigents. To do so, there is a need to establish objective criteria to determine indigent status, so funds can be administered fairly. Indigent funds are not established in all jurisdictions, but about half of the informants noted that their State has some provision for indigents. In New Mexico, the indigent fund pays for half the monthly fee, plus the installation and removal. However, judges sometimes make determinations on vague bases and there have been legislative efforts

to systemize use of the indigent fund via more widely recognized indicators of poverty level used by the Federal Government.

- **Recommendation: Indigent Fund**
  States should make some provision for low income DWI offenders, but no specific suggestions were offered by the expert panel. In most programs where there is an indigent set aside, a fee is captured from all installations or monthly lease fees to establish this pool of funds. Other suggestions included diverting some portion of alcohol excise taxes for this purpose. If a fund is established, experience in New Mexico strongly suggests that some standard test of indigency is needed to help the courts or licensing authority determine eligibility for these funds.

- **Anticircumvention Protocols**
  As noted previously, anticircumvention protocols (designed to prevent a person from starting the vehicle without first passing a BAC test) are features built into all the devices, while any State adopting interlock devices that meet the NHTSA Model Specifications can be assured that circumvention protection capabilities in the device are present, it is still up to the State to require all service providers operating within the State always to have those circumvention features active. This became an issue in recent years when it was determined that some vendors tried to gain market advantage by advertising their devices to offenders as "blow and go"—meaning no inconvenience of providing anticircumvention sequences, such as hum codes or suck/blow sequences.
  Most respondents reported circumvention issues as a rare problem; others reported it to be an occasional problem. All of those States reporting it as rare require activation of the interlock's hum code, suck/blow, breath temperature criterion, or other anticircumvention protocols. Without those protocols, circumvention can be achieved by providing a bogus air sample, or by physically bypassing the interlock. There is general interest in requiring noncircumventable devices and much interest in having interlocks that can identify the blower. States that actively require anticircumvention protocols report that use of other vehicles is the most typical circumvention. Some commented that the easiest way to circumvent the interlock (other than driving a different vehicle) is popping the clutch on a vehicle with a manual transmission. Arizona has, at least in the past, regarded failure to take a rolling retest as a circumvention attempt. All

jurisdictions regarded intentional circumvention and/or disabling the interlock to be a serious violation that can result in a variety of sanctions.

While we ordinarily assume the most common circumvention is via driving a different vehicle, a recent attempt in New Mexico to estimate the rate of circumventing while using the interlock vehicle found 25 percent of repeat DWI arrests occurred with the interlock vehicle (Marques et al., 2009, in press). This likely means that either circumvention was not active or the driver bypassed the interlock.

- **Recommendation: Anticircumvention Protocols**

  All jurisdictions should require that anticircumvention blow sequences (or protocols) be activated at all times. Providers serving the State as interlock installers should risk loss of State certification for knowingly disabling these protections. There continue to be reports (including local news reports with video) that some service providers may be disabling their anticircumvention controls. Responsible providers have reported that some local service providers actively promote interlocks on the public airwaves as "blow and go," implying no bothersome hum tones, toot sequences or other kinds of anticircumvention protocols. States should have regulations that prohibit these practices.

- **Vendor Responsibilities**

  Providers and/or manufacturers that operate in a State should be required to comply with established expectations for a responsible business and must serve as an agent of State policy. Accordingly, the State should be clear about the expectations and performance standards. Some States may be stricter than others in assuring providers meet minimum standards.

  In Colorado, interlock devices are approved by the Department of Health and Environment, while the Department of Revenue requires performance bonds for companies to do business in the State. Providers in Colorado must report weekly to the State on ALL drivers via data downloads, and must develop contracts with each driver to assure that he/she will conform to the State requirements. Providers also must report customer complaints. If providers have poor service that is not corrected, the State may cease to accept their driver contracts. This can ultimately result in contract termination and a charge against the bond if not resolved satisfactorily. The Department of Revenue is the central agency in Colorado for this administrative program. The State is working on a multi-agency cross communication strategy among courts, therapy, DMV and probation. This seems to be a well thought through system of regulation.

Pennsylvania seems to have a very thorough inspection program that requires any modifications to the certified device to be reported promptly. Arizona conducts annual checks and unannounced checks when warranted. Few States maintain an active surprise inspection protocol of service facilities, although most have some provision for sanctioning providers when problems become known. New Mexico announces annual inspections and also conducts random visits to providers and investigates complaints. However, a counter view suggests that providers are rarely, if ever, sanctioned with any consequence stronger than a letter from the probation department. One respondent believed that the State regulatory bodies must be more active in sanctioning irresponsible operators, since such companies can damage the industry reputation. Another provider contrasted the inspection processes in 3 States and noted that California requires virtually nothing, Texas everything, and Arizona only paperwork. He sees the Texas model as favorable. In Florida, reporting is comprehensive and includes blow attempts, violations, warnings, aborts, and miles driven. Also, Florida conducts unannounced site visits to inspect records and procedures at least once a year. It should be noted that legislative revisions may have changed some of these practices by the time of publication.

In managing vendors, States should be aware that wide varieties of vendor/State arrangements can be found: sole providers, noncompete market segments (in Florida, one company services the north end and one the south end of the State) or an open market (like New Mexico, with uses up to seven different providers). In most cases, when the interlock service provider is not a dedicated business (that does only interlock work) it may be because there are too few customers. Accordingly, side line interlock businesses are becoming more common, as more States begin startup programs. Often, until business opportunities develop, the stand-alone interlock companies cannot afford to open dedicated facilities. Quebec provides interlock service to very rural areas by working through a single auto services company that operates an extensive network of stores.

- **Recommendation: Vendor Responsibilities and Arrangements** This is an area about which several States appear to have given considerable thought and have applied resources. While the number of States providing information was limited, it appears that several States have active inspection programs and could help advise others. Some of the more experienced States appear to be Florida, Colorado, Maryland, Texas, Virginia, and Pennsylvania. The number of interlock service providers operating in the State is less important than assuring the quality of procedures and reporting to which each provider must adhere. States should be willing to de-license providers if they fail to comply with State regulations for reporting. This, in turn, requires that States establish attainable requirements and promulgate clear instructions for all vendors operating within their borders. The biggest problem with the use of multi-service companies for interlock may be the inherent conflict of interest between serving as an agent of the government (for interlock) and the more natural inclination to serve customers regarding their other products.

3. Standardization of Reporting and Information Flow

Science relies on "operational" definitions so all can have a common understanding of the meaning of technical words when communicating or reading research reports. Operational definitions specify the precise conditions regarding events that have occurred. Companies that have produced an alcohol control device in response to market forces are unlikely to be concerned about using the same definitions and language as their competitors. However, when the market achieves some greater degree of maturity, issues such as uniform use of language and procedures can rise to a level of concern. In 2009, the interlock industry appears to be emerging from years of immaturity to a place where greater internal order may be needed for governments to use their products most efficiently.

Different companies report different types of DWI offender interlock performance information to the monitoring authority. The problem is not constrained just to which factors they choose to report and how they arrange the information. The companies are not constrained to any common standard of what constitutes a breath test, much less circumvention or other violations. Two research groups represented at the expert panel, Westat and PIRE, have independently conducted comparative analyses of data log files from different companies and both reported on the difficulty of comparing interlock log files across vendors, since there is great inconsistency in the definition of events; that is, there are no operational definitions that all companies recognize. An important goal at the end-user level should be to have a common understanding of what a report means and what each reported item represents operationally. To achieve such a goal, we will need to adhere to a common standard. The report formats will only be as valid as the underlying assumptions that feed them.

- **Interlock Company Report to the Monitoring Authorities**
  Today, there are no recognized reporting standards other than those developed by the manufacturers. Several manufacturers do a very good job of condensing a lot of information into a concise, readable format, but the States themselves should decide what they want in the monthly reports, what the reported information actually means and how to use the information. In the short term, States need to be familiar with the report content and format offered by different manufacturers. However, while comparing those reports, there also will need to be attention given to the definitions of data elements (e.g., not all companies have the same criteria for the words “circumvention,” ”time lapse failure,” “failed retest,” etc.). In addition, the problem is larger than the information that is received and whether it is consistent or sensible for the person having to interpret the report. The responsible person in charge of the State program should be able to understand how the meaning of those report labels might differ from company to company.
  Regarding reports, some key informants suggested that an ideal law might require a period of clean time before full reinstatement is possible. This topic is covered in the next section, but if there is to be any kind of consequence to the offenders for their interlock breath test record, it presumes that there are coherent regularly provided reports and that someone monitors and takes action on those reports. Informants advise that this is not always the case. Some interlock service providers complain that, in many cases, little is done with the reports when they are made available, or the authority requires no reports. For the reports to do much good, some authority should receive and evaluate performance. One representative of an interlock company reported at a recent meeting that at least two States explicitly request interlock companies to NOT bother them with

reports because it creates some expectation that they will do something with them, and they have no spare resources.

- **General Recommendation: Report Standards**
  At the panel meeting, it was suggested that national standards should be developed with model specifications for program reporting and report format. It would be worthwhile to have common reporting elements. If that were to ever happen, it is still likely way in the future. The format of the report provided to the State Monitoring Authority would need to be dependent on the type of information captured in the interlock device. We recommend that technical staff familiar with electronic and BAC test equipment in each State attempt to understand how and what information is captured and stored in each interlock that is approved for use in each State.
  The specification of required data elements might best be included as part of a future revision of the Model Specifications for Breath Alcohol Ignition Interlock Devices, which specifies minimal device standards – a separate issue entirely than minimal program features. Alternatively, these features could be proposed as a set of recommendations. The State should make adequate resources available to the program monitors, so offenders are part of the information loop and are advised when their performance does not meet program expectations.
- **Specific Recommendations: Report Format, Content, and Frequency**
  Panel members discussed several things that would help make an offender's performance report more meaningful and to facilitate communication across jurisdictions. High among the suggestions were to firm up the language and use words that have common definitions and to avoid using words that appear to reach conclusions before the monitoring authority itself comes to a decision.
  Specific suggestions noted by members of the panel included the following:

1. Use value-neutral wording:
   a. The words used in reports today often pose problems. When a service provider uses the word "violation," the private sector is passing a judgment on the way in which

the monitoring entity should regard the report. This would not be a big problem if there were not a sea of nuance surrounding many positive breath test results. Therefore, value-neutral wording would be preferable. The report should summarize "events," and all reports should reflect a similar neutral tone. The interpretation is up to the authority, not the private company. The log file is an event recorder, and "events" should be reported.

   b. The header on a monthly report should NOT be a "compliance" report; it simply should be a report. Compliance is a judgment for the authority to render, based on the evidence presented. When an interlock successfully locks out a positive BAC test, the driver did not drive impaired. Therefore, some view the driver as compliant, since the driver was prevented from driving impaired; others viewed the driver as noncompliant, since the driver attempted to operate the vehicle with a positive BAC. We need to define some of these words carefully; labels acquire meanings. Judges who are presented with reports of "violations," or evidence of "noncompliance," could have their options constrained a priori by the interlock company.
   c. There should be a standard operational definition of the word "circumvention," because this is another word that implies a conclusion.

2. If judgments are rendered, define them operationally:
   a. If the word "violation" were to be retained in monthly reports, the event that reflects a "violation" should be maximally useful to a prosecutor since he/she will need solid evidence. For example, a breath test that is elevated and results in a lockout is hard to describe as a clear violation, if a breath test 5 minutes later is passed easily. The initial test could reflect transient mouth alcohol from food or mouthwash. (Many ripe fruits contain a small amount of alcohol that can be sufficient to cause a false positive, due to mouth alcohol.) Such events should not be reported as a violation. Some of these types of problems could be overcome with better interpretational algorithms by the manufacturers.

   b. Any failed test should be followed by a required retest, in order to improve the confidence of judgments made by the monitoring authority.
3. Assure shared access to information by all divisions of government that need it:
   a. To actively monitor an offender's BAC performance, a method of e-mail notification could ensue when "red flag events" (significant problems) occur. A query-based or online retrieval system also could serve the needs of those court entities who believe they should know immediately when an offender/ driver has had a performance event defined as a violation, circumvention, or noncompliance.
   b. Interlock offenders who travel across State boundaries potentially pose difficulties in how States view interlock licenses. For example, in New Mexico, an ignition interlock license permits driving, but the DWI revocation officially is still on the books during the interlock restriction. A New Mexico offender with an interlock license was arrested for speeding in Washington while driving an interlock vehicle. The Washington officer checked and found his license officially revoked and sent him to jail for driving while suspended. It took a couple of days and much effort before the situation could be resolved. States need to set up rules through the Interstate Compact for Offender Tracking to deal with these cross-State issues.
4. Require consistent notations for bypass or other exceptions due to vehicle repair work:
   a. Vehicles can be expected to need maintenance service, whether or not there is an interlock in operation. Third-party maintenance (TPM) can be expected to be performed by automotive service technicians and they will need some way to start the vehicle that bypasses the interlock. There is a need to better code or approve legitimate vehicle service work by TPM entities. For example, Draeger sends a code to a TPM, so the vehicle can be started without the interlock. This code expires within an hour of issuance. Apparently, a similar method

is used by ACS and perhaps other vendors. When such service requests are submitted to ACS, the company calls the TPM to verify legitimacy and then provides a temporary override code. Smart Start requires an advance call-in. The vehicle circumvention that occurs is recorded as a disconnect violation, but the record is later marked as an approved exception. Power disconnect is a difficult interpretation problem. If those events enter into the log file, the event recorder should be able to mark them as legitimate service episodes. This may not be occurring in some cases. Finally, have the vendors considered the effect of this legitimization process on owners/operators who are skilled enough to repair their own vehicles but do not work in a garage or do repairs commercially? States should develop a consistent set of protocols for making decisions about authorized overrides or bypass.

5. Establish consistent frequency of reports:
    a. The frequency of reporting is still a topic of some dispute. The monitoring authority ideally should have online access to offender interlock performance at any time desired, to perform queries about a particular offender. However, for the routine notification process, most authorities prefer 30-day reports (when they prefer anything at all), and that is the recommendation of this report. Comments relating to report frequency were reviewed by the expert panel or key informants. The following issues were raised.
    b. For those judged compliant, some believed it is acceptable to establish an interval longer than 30 days. This was disputed by others, however, who regard 30 days as a preferred standard.
    c. One contrary view suggested that there is no need to wait 30 days to obtain data—abstinence monitoring advocates would prefer receiving data in realtime. There were disputes on this issue that related to the central purpose of the interlock—see below on philosophical differences. Some offender cases were thought to require more frequent review, due to public risk exposure.

d. One or more panelists believed two report formats should be developed for two (or more) levels of offender severity. This suggests that the content and frequency of reporting should reflect perceived offender risk. Currently, some States extract specific data elements from the vendor database for their own monitoring purposes.
e. A quality assurance protocol should be put in place to ensure that reports are received by the responsible authority. Perhaps a database could be established to indicate that certain people have not had reports reviewed or received. It would be a way of officially flagging where the responsibility lies for monitoring.
f. Protocols are needed for monitoring providers/vendors, as their full cooperation is critical to making the programs work. Some States such as Maryland achieve this by making periodic inspections on short notice.

- **General Recommendation: Report Format, Content, and Frequency**

  Accurate, timely, understandable reports are the most important way for the responsible authority to check on the performance of an offender. It would seem that there should be some form of sign-off protocol required, so offender violations are noted. Reports can be viewed online or on paper, but they should be reviewed by someone who must measure offender performance against State or court standards.

  It would be worthwhile for someone in each State to accumulate all current and planned report formats for equipment approved by the State, along with the underlying data that is reported, to compare the accuracy, commonality, and adequacy of reporting against a consensus standard for minimal information and expected actions. Having the ability to invoke prompt consequences is a cardinal principal of behavior change theory, and the longer the delay between the violation or behavior, the less effective will be the counter response for adjusting that behavior.

  Determining which divisions of government have a natural interest in offender performance reports could be agreed upon early, when new programs are being planned.

- **Minimal Vehicle Use Requirements or Confirmation Protocols**
  There ought to be some method to assure that offenders are not just parking the interlock vehicle as a way to comply with a State requirement, and then driving an alternate vehicle for all driving except interlock service calls. Some States such as New Mexico are requiring that odometers be read during the service calls. Alternatively, an estimate of vehicle use is available in all programs by enumerating the number of times and dates when the vehicle was started (these data are recorded on the interlock event record). The latter is the method of choice by Maryland, and 50 starts per month is the required minimum. Most States do not have protocols for assuring minimal vehicle use. Many key informants believed this is a worthwhile check on compliance with the interlock program and could be as simple as noting odometer readings each month as New Mexico does now. Alternatively, it would be easy for the monthly report format to note the number of startup tests and the duration of each ride, until engine shut down, yielding a number of starts and mean trip length. This should be one of the reporting services provided by the vendor.
  - **Recommendation: Minimal Vehicle Use Indicators**
    States should require that the monthly report include some estimate of vehicle use to document offender driving. This is especially important in States that require the interlock as a condition of license reinstatement and/or States that impose on drivers a period (e.g., 3 to 6 months) of zero BAC elevations prior to reinstatement.

    A question was raised during the expert panel meeting regarding the requirement for minimum use of vehicle (e.g., to preclude parking the vehicle and waiting out the interlock requirement), and that was: Can there be a legal sanction for not using the vehicle? The answer was that it serves more as a way to bring in an offender for an administrative review session. According to most informants, this is used more often for reporting, rather than sanctioning for non-use of the vehicle. Of course, the motive for imposing this reporting requirement is because non-use of the interlock vehicle raises concern that an offender is using an alternative vehicle.

4. Program Compliance, Noncompliance, and Interlock Removal

Having reviewed issues surrounding the issuance of reports to the interlock monitoring authority, it is time to review the major topic that will be of interest to those who read those reports—BAC ignition interlock lockouts, procedural violations, and what to do about them. It is in regard to these decisions that the philosophical differences in program orientation have the greatest implications and that topic is discussed at the end of this section.

There are three general categories of noncompliance: repeated BAC lockouts, procedural failures such as not taking retests when required, and starting the vehicle without first passing a BAC test such as circumvention (e.g., bypassing the interlock by "hot-wiring" the starter). In addition, some States have added a requirement for some minimal amount of vehicle use (e.g., as detected by either the number of start up tests or odometer readings), in order to preclude the possibility that an interlock stipulated offender is not letting the vehicle sit without being used between required service visits, while perhaps using a noninterlock vehicle.

- **Procedural Violations**
  Procedural violations and circumventions are less complicated problems than BAC lockouts. Some procedural violations are as minor as not taking a final running retest prior to parking the vehicle because the trip had ended. On the other extreme, intentional circumvention (via hot-wiring or delivering a bogus breath sample) is a much more serious violation. Procedural violations are less common then BAC lockouts. When procedural violations represent an active intent to defy the program's rules, it requires the State to consider what consequences should follow. Other procedural violations include failure to take requested retests, failed BAC retests after an initial start and failure to pull over and stop the vehicle after failed retests.
  - **Recommendation: Procedural Violations and Circumventions**
    The occurrence of intentional circumvention may warrant the Monitoring Authority to consider removing the offender from the interlock program or to retain the offender while also invoking a more restrictive form of monitoring, such as house arrest, SCRAM, or other types of sanctions that can be applied through court authority. Procedural violations such as failure to take a requested retest are sometimes explained by the offender, e.g., expecting to arrive at his or her destination just a few minutes

after the device called for a retest. In these cases, a plan for sanctioning should reflect the pattern and apparent severity.

- **Understanding and Dealing With BAC Lockouts**
The proportion of offenders testing positive for alcohol on interlock BAC tests is one of the few program-related issues on which there is evaluation information. Studies at PIRE have analyzed in total over 50 million BAC tests across four different U.S. and Canadian programs, provided by over 20,000 offenders. The results generally are similar. After 6 or more months of interlock controlled driving, between 60 to 90 percent of all interlockusing offenders have some positive (>.02 g/dL) breath tests or lockouts. Evidence shows that those with the highest rates of positive BAC tests also have the highest rate of DWI recidivism after the interlock has been removed (Marques et al., 1999, 2001, 2003b, 2003c, 2009). Therefore, having a plan to deal with offenders who log high rates of lockouts is necessary. The type of plan imposed should be attentive to the interlock program's attitude about locked out starts due to BAC; that is, whether the program sees its role broadly to control impaired driving, or whether it sees the interlock as a tool to enforce abstinence. Regardless, the evaluation information is germane to both approaches.
BAC lockouts can occur any time of day, but the time of day when most of these positive tests occur is during the first morning start-up. This might seem surprising, but it is a consistent finding in all four data sets evaluated, and is generally interpreted as a result of alcohol levels that are still up from a prior night of drinking. The body processes about three-quarters or more of a drink per hour, so it can take more than 7 or 8 hours after heavy evening drinking for a BAC to decline below the lockout point. Furthermore, in all of the studies conducted, the rate of locked-out tests decline as experience with the interlock proceeds (e.g., the rates are twice as high in the first two months as they are 6 months later). Accordingly, programs that intend to impose strong punitive sanctions for any lockouts need to take into consideration that DWI offenders may not promptly attain control of their drinking, or fully separate the timing of their drinking and driving. After a few months of experience with the interlock, the rate of positive tests and lockouts decline, even though the total number of tests taken does not decline (i.e., driving holds constant, failed BAC test rates decline). While learning is likely a factor, it is important to remember that the studies of interlock BAC log files also have

determined that those with higher rates of failed BAC tests (morning tests or all tests) have higher rates of postinterlock recidivism. Performance on the BAC tests is an important window into the post-interlock risk status.

- **Recommendation: BAC Lockouts**
  Because the evidence clearly shows that higher rates of BAC lockouts are predictive of DWI risk, it is recommended that the monitoring authority begin developing a tracking system for each offender with the first report. For example, those with more than 1 percent of all start tests that are lockouts, or those who have so few start tests of any kind that might suggest non-use of the vehicle, should be tracked and perhaps called in for a discussion. One possibility is to set criteria at the outset that might trigger a warning letter or a call from a treatment provider if State statutes support such an approach.

- **Different Consequences for BAC Levels and High Rates of Lockouts**
  Many panel members believe that the interlock BAC test performance should be used to scale the interlock program response to the offender and be used to set consequences that reflect apparent risk to the driving public.
  Some States already use the BAC test reports as a criterion for evaluating offender drinking status.
  In Colorado, one year of interlock time is added for 3 consecutive months of locked out BAC tests in a 12-month period.
  By contrast, in Pennsylvania three BAC test lockouts above set point, one retest violation, or one tampering requires the offender to report for a device reset (which costs money for the service call), but no further penalties are imposed.
  The Michigan program distinguishes between minor violations and major violations. Minor violations in Michigan are defined as missing monitoring appointments or having three elevated BAC violations in a monitoring period. Each minor violation adds 3 months of interlock time. With major violations (defined as three minor violations in a period, an OWI [operating while impaired] arrest or a rolling retest failure >.04 g/dL), the offender is removed from interlock and license revocation is re-instituted.

In New Mexico, positive tests are considered a violation, but whether a penalty is imposed as a result is up to the judge and is usually based on the offender's pattern of past behavior.

In the California program, the respondent noted that elevated tests are considered evidence that the device is working properly and no violation is charged. By contrast, in the California program, noncompliance (tampering or circumvention) will result in being removed from the interlock program.

In Florida, the consequence for one BAC violation (>.051 g/dL) requires that the offender report to the program monitor; for two elevated tests, the offender must report to the monthly DWI program. All elevated tests are coded as offenses.

A survey respondent from New York strongly urged extension for violations, but as yet, no such provision was in place in his jurisdiction.

West Virginia's approach involves a demerit system that "costs" offenders additional interlock time for various violations based on number and levels of elevated tests. A survey respondent from Texas noted that interlock extension is possible. This may be a likely option in many judicial programs, within the limits of the enabling legislation.

Maryland currently has no provision for extending an offender's time on the interlock based on performance. Many survey respondents who noted that their States did not have a statute providing for an extension of the required interlock period based on reported performance believed the extension was a good idea.

Virginia requires 6 months of violation-free interlock, and if there is a BAC violation during that 6-month period, the clock resets. New Mexico does not do this now, but respondents liked the idea of compliance-based removal. They also expressed some concern that it might be burdensome to the licensing agency. No extension is possible right now in Florida, but they are recommending legislation to reduce required interlock time based on good performance. Reportedly, other States with some provision for extension include, at a minimum, South Carolina, Arizona, Illinois, and Massachusetts.

Finally, although statutes differ across States, we know that the language of a statute does not necessarily mean it is implemented as stated.

- **Recommendation: Interlock Extensions Due to BAC and Lockouts**

  The data in the interlock log file should be used proactively to improve road safety. The decision to extend in the above States will be at least partly dependent on the record of breath tests stored in the interlock device. Examples of the interlock log events that could trigger an extension include skipped retests, failed retests, circumventions, and a pattern of elevated BAC tests. (In order to have confidence in the legitimacy of these conclusions, it is necessary to have good reporting, clear definitions of "violations" and good information flow).

  There was general agreement at the expert panel meeting that, in most cases, there is no public safety benefit gained by removing someone from the interlock program for frequent lockout BAC tests. Nor does it make sense to award an unrestricted license to someone who has a continuing pattern of elevated BAC tests. There was some suggestion that administrative sanctions (via the licensing authority) are more straightforward to apply than criminal sanctions, but a growing demand for administrative hearings could make this more problematic. Not all agreed with this possible concern, but most of the panel agreed that intentional procedural violations are a more serious problem.

- **Alcohol-Free Performance Before Issuance of an Unrestricted License**

  There was strong concern that unrestricted licenses not be issued to offenders who show a repeated pattern of BAC lockouts, especially during the last several months of required interlock use. Interlock BAC test records are required in order to enforce such a requirement. The more difficult problem is how to set reasonable criteria and, here again, the approach must reflect the philosophical views of the interlock program: enforcing offender abstinence or minimizing public exposure to risk.

  - **Recommendation: Alcohol-Free Period Prior to Relicensing**

    In these recommendations, the authors suggest a middle path under which offenders must attain some level of interlock performance in the final 3 to 6 months of the interlock period that reflects continued vehicle use and no alcohol related lockouts.

- **Philosophical Differences Regarding Elevated Interlock Breath Tests**

A large number of States (or courts) regard even one or two lockouts (successfully blocked positive BAC start-up attempts) as a violation. Many panelists believed having a very strict consequence for elevated BAC tests early in the interlock program period is not a good idea, since it is at odds with the potential educational function of an interlock, especially because it is such a common occurrence. Early in an interlock period, people may be just learning about BAC curves and durations. And as noted above, 60 to 90 percent of all offenders have at least one lockout. The initial recommendation that was brought to the expert panel meeting was that interlock programs should allow some number of elevated BAC lockouts per period, initially to allow for learning, and then phase in consequences that help to shape the desired behavior and attain separation between drinking and driving. It was further recommended that, nearing the conclusion of the interlock period, offenders should be required to have 3 to 6 months of no elevated BAC tests in order to avoid an interlock extension. The regular use of the interlock vehicle should be monitored carefully to assure that a requirement that there be no failed BAC test results does not unintentionally encourage the use of an alternative vehicle. The attitude was that we should not impose conditions that are so demanding that they encourage offenders to abandon the interlock and choose to drive illegally instead.

Not everyone on the panel agreed with this view. Some of the panelists, especially some of the judges present, argued that no lockout BAC tests should be tolerated. They argued that abstinence is a powerful requirement that goads behavior change. Not punishing positive BACs, it was argued, might be seen as contrary to that judicial philosophy and a tacit approval of interlock offenders who blow positive BAC tests. Not all judges agreed with this position, but it was an undercurrent that defined a difference among panelists. Even some who generally preferred the public safety approach (let them learn and but keep raising the bar) agreed that the abstinence requirement help judges to encourage behavior change. Considering the prevalence of positive tests (about 60 to 90% of all DWI offenders on interlock), the manner in which programs address these tests is very significant.

Another view is that the interlock device, by design, provides a monitoring system in which BAC tests above the lockout point (usually .025 g/dL) produce an immediate sanction—an inability to start the vehicle, a swift and certain consequence with significant driver inconvenience. Because of this primary consequence, imposed by the device, a court-ordered sanction is thought to be unnecessary and a potential interference in the early stages of learning for someone who needs to adjust his or her behavior to live with the interlock. The primary interlock penalty—lockout—is imposed without any personnel cost to the court or administrative system. As long as the offender does not attempt to circumvent the interlock, the public risk exposure is limited. Interlock research has demonstrated a pattern of BAC tests that suggest that something akin to learning occurs in the early stages of interlock use because offenders tend to reduce their BAC lockouts over the first several months on these programs. In addition, the BAC test records might be the resource needed to draw a distinction between lower and higher risk offenders. Accordingly, it would be cost-efficient to let the interlock have its effect on offender behavior before imposing higher cost sanctions (such as jail, house arrest, or real-time monitoring) that may require the expenditure of court probation resources. Further, overly severe restrictions may inadvertently encourage unlicensed driving, and that approach would be contrary to the public safety goal of installing and using more interlocks. A derivative belief is that, for many offenders, modification of drinking-driving behavior is most likely to occur with moderate sanctions—initially just the annoyance of the failure of the vehicle to start, later with the threat that the required time driving with an interlock might be extended or even a court threat to require more restrictive monitoring.

- **Should There be Two Different Types of Interlock Programs?** Court versus licensing programs? High-risk versus low-risk offenders? How would the distinction be made for tracking toward either of the two programs? Beyond the core differences about the attainment of abstinence as a primary goal versus installing more interlocks as a primary goal, there was widespread agreement among panel members about other elements of an interlock program that are needed to create programs that run well and are effective. Many of these issues have been discussed earlier in this report.

  The expert panel showed great interest in addressing philosophical differences about the question of abstinence. It was an animated discussion. One option may be to accept both approaches as being legitimate in the management of different types of DWI offenders and to promulgate two different types of ignition interlock program guidelines, depending on the requirements imposed on the offender. If this approach is adopted, it would warrant an effectiveness evaluation of the relative safety benefit by method, after adjusting for offender risk and compliance. This is a researchable question; one that does not need to be decided on the basis of tradition and guesswork. The New Mexico judicial administrative hybrid program has elements of both approaches and results now demonstrate clear effectiveness of the New Mexico program (Roth et al., 2007a, Roth et al., 2007b, Roth et al., 2009). While there has never been a study of whether hybrid programs are superior, the question could be evaluated if there was a willing court system. Among those on the expert panel, those focused primarily on public safety espoused the idea that reducing drunk driving is a more practical and attainable goal than curing alcohol dependence. However, both approaches may be warranted and there is reason to think they can work well together.

On the other hand, the court system has its own traditions and is a core component of safety enforcement. The interlock, since its introduction as a tool to help reduce alcoholrelated crashes and injury, has been embraced by court systems throughout the United States; in fact, some courts experimented with interlocks as DWI interventions before there were State laws. Both historically and practically, the courts play an important role in public safety by imposing restrictions on individuals who pose risks to the public. In accordance with that responsibility, courts often require known DWI offenders, particularly repeat offenders, to abstain completely from drinking alcohol. Because the courts can impose fines and threaten freedom, they have considerable leverage over offender behavior, and often the courts view any elevated breath tests in the alcohol ignition interlock log file as evidence of noncompliance by offenders who have "abstinence from alcohol" as one of their conditions of probation.

The fear expressed by some expert panel members is that the abstinence requirement, if it were to become widely imposed on DWI offenders, could transform a pragmatic, self-funded, drunk-driving preventative intervention into a tool for BAC monitoring. An abstinence requirement would render each of those lockouts due to BAC as a "violation" of the court order and, therefore, subject to further sanctioning. However, road safety related to alcohol does not require abstinence; it just requires there be no drinking and driving. This difference reflects frames of reference between the natural interests of the criminal justice system and public safety system. These differences are very similar to the ones that divide the medical care system and the public health system. In the former, the individual receives the focus of attention; in the latter, community safety and public health receive the focus of attention. Both are important; both are legitimate; so we need to find a middle way.

- **Recommendation: Two Types of Interlock Programs?**
  There is no consensus recommendation available to answer this question. One possibility is for State legislation to be written in a way that provides for two levels of risk in the designation of alcohol offenders. Higher risk offenders might be expected to meet a higher standard of public risk protection through some form of enforced abstinence while lower risk offenders simply could be processed through an interlock program without abstinence expectations, or perfectly clean BAC test records, at least initially. The problem with mandating abstinence is that ending alcohol dependence often requires more than a stern lecture and a strong sanction. There are few interlock programs that run concurrent with alcohol treatment programs, and even targeted treatment success among DWI offenders is very modest. A meta-analysis (a study of studies) showed that court-ordered mandatory treatment yields an improvement of about 8 to 9 percent (Wells-Parker, Bangert-Drowns, McMillen, & Williams, 1995). No doubt, success at ending alcohol dependence would end the alcohol impaired driving risk of high-risk offenders more definitively. The majority of evidence shows that alcohol interlocks suppress impaired driving only while the devices are installed. The safest approach may be to maintain the interlock unless successful control of alcohol use can be attained.

5. Linkage to Treatment

As noted in the Foundational Statement earlier in this document, after first protecting the community, a secondary objective is to help rehabilitate the alcohol offender when possible. Most DWI intervention programs, at least those for multiple offenders, require some form of alcohol counseling or treatment. Use of the words "counseling" and "treatment" do not have consensus definitions, but counseling is sometimes seen as a lighter form of intervention than treatment. Treatment usually implies a behavior change intervention in a structured program, or one with a treatment plan, provided by a licensed professional with advanced degrees. Both approaches often use self-help support groups outside of the programs. Court-ordered attendance at fellowship-based self-help groups, such as Alcoholics Anonymous, is deemed helpful to some, but widely criticized by others since coerced attendance is not in keeping with the idea of self-help.

- **Interlock BAC Data and Alcohol Treatment**
  In typical DWI programs that provided intervention services long before there was an interlock option available, alcohol treatment services often were required prior to relicensing. Today, in many States, entry into an interlock program is the final step toward unrestricted driving. Many State programs that require alcohol behavior change intervention still require treatment before an offender can get behind the wheel again (e.g., before interlock). States perhaps should re-sequence these events so that the offender is driving with interlock controls while still receiving counseling or treatment services. The interlock program and the stored BAC test information can provide the therapist with objective information about DWI client behavior. If counseling overlaps the interlock program, the nature of the client-therapist relationship might be strengthened in a way that eventually better protects the public.
  The above arrangement, if implemented, could serve the needs of both the abstinence-first and the public safety-first programs. Both approaches seek the same outcome – safer roads and reduced risk of public hazard due to impaired driving.
  - **Recommendation: Interlock BAC Log Data and Treatment**
    All State DWI programs that require interlocks and a period of treatment prior to full relicensing should consider integrating the two so that personal behavior change counselors or therapists can review monthly data log files and help the offender gain better control of drinking. This is appropriate for both abstinence and public safety programs. The interlock is underexploited as a bridge technology, and it could link the health and criminal aspects of alcohol problems more effectively.
- **Does a Court Order of Abstinence Impose a Treatment Obligation on the Government?**

Outside the context of DWI courts, where offenders are actively monitored for drinking status and supported by treatment resources, a court-ordered requirement for abstinence may not come with much counseling or other behavior change supports. Should payment for these services be a public responsibility if the court orders abstinence? Court-ordered or coerced change can create the incentive for many to work harder at self-change, but self-change is a difficult thing to achieve (even with behavior change support); failure is more common than success. Judges point out that their court order to remain abstinent often follow a period of required alcohol treatment. Most alcohol treatment participants today are court-ordered (Weisner, Matzger, Tam, & Schmidt, 2002). However, as demonstrated by the largest multi-center trial of alcoholism treatment outcome ever undertaken, Project MATCH (1997), alcohol treatment interventions do not lead to sustained abstinence for the majority of clients beyond the first 6 post-treatment months. DWI court programs may help support offender behavior change. However, if a court desires abstinence but cannot offer a DWI court program, a compromise approach may be more attainable, in which regular treatment services are made integral with the interlock, so that monthly breath test information from the interlock becomes part of the treatment conversation between the offender and the therapist.

- **Recommendation: If Abstinence, Then Treatment**
  The Panel did not provide clear guidance on whether judges should impose an abstinence requirement. Courts have the right to impose any fair requirement on offenders, especially if those requirements serve the public interest. It is clear that changing a DWI offender into a citizen whose drinking is fully under control is in the public interest, and there are many alcohol counseling or treatment programs that serve offenders and can help guide attainment of those changes. If the court imposes an abstinence requirement, however, the court should make some provision to help the offender attain abstinence, since behavior change is fundamentally about learning new skills. It may be worthwhile for the State to examine the feasibility of extending the use of interlock program indigent funds to help those in need of alcohol treatment services that can be integrated into an interlock program. Better control over drinking by DWI offenders is in the public interest.

- **Some Examples of Treatment Components**
  In West Virginia, all participants in the interlock program also must enroll in the Alcohol Safety Treatment Program. Once an offender is enrolled, BAC readings from the interlock can be reported to the treatment provider. If the treatment provider decides to drop an offender for program violations, the offender is removed from the interlock program as well. This is a novel way to link the safety aspects of the interlock to the rehabilitative features of a treatment program. It might yield a better safety benefit if a more restrictive sanction (a SCRAM bracelet or electronic monitoring for house arrest) is available for failures as a way to step-up the monitoring, rather than stepping it down by interlock program removal. Many States report interest in treatment-linked programs, but few seem to have one that is keyed specifically to the interlock. Colorado has an interest in developing a program based on the SIP (Support for Interlock Planning) model (Timken & Marques, 2001a; 2001b). In Maryland, the Medical Review Board can order offenders onto interlocks and set the conditions for re-licensure. The Virginia Alcohol Safety Action Program (VASAP) has direct treatment links. In Virginia, case managers report interlock BAC violations to the treatment providers, who then take action. The case managers are a center point of action between the offenders, the courts, the treatment and the interlock provider. Many States with DWI or drug courts use the interlock as a tool to help goad behavior change. Florida does not have a treatment link, but they do require a counseling session for a first violation; for a second violation, they must report to the DWI program monthly for the duration of their installation (this is not treatment – more like extended monitoring).
  - **Recommendation: Treatment-Interlock Linkage**
    States are exploring various methods of linking the interlock and treatment elements. Other States interested in pursuing a linkage model should contact those in some of the above States to learn more and determine whether those models can serve as a basis for treatment linkage models. There is a largely unexploited opportunity to merge the interlock program with a counseling component, whether full treatment or a low cost motivational intervention like SIP is being used. It seems logical that a thoughtful convergence in this area could be very cost effective. However, we are aware of no evaluation information on how well

these programs are working. Most treatment or rehabilitation programs for DWI offenders are separate and stand-alone services.

6. Key Differences in Court Programs and Motor Vehicle Authority Programs

There are several key differences between administrative interlock programs managed by the licensing authority and judicial programs managed by the courts. A considerable number of these differences have been discussed already in different contexts. The major differences with respect to interlock implementation and monitoring are as follows.

Administrative programs are centralized, can be extended easily to all eligible convicted offenders and the programs can be implemented promptly. On the other hand, the consequences it can impose when offenders are in violation are more limited. The licensing authority can withhold the license but, without the court, cannot impose stronger non-licensing sanctions.

In addition, administrative programs that order the installation of interlocks run the risk of having to manage many administrative appeal hearings without adequate staffing.

Court programs can ensure offender compliance with interlock orders more easily, since the court can impose strict sanctions, such as jail time or house arrest. Accordingly, judicial programs can attain higher rates of installation. On the down side, the courts are independent from each other and it is difficult to get hundreds of courts to implement interlock programs and adopt common practices. In addition, probation resources already are overextended in many jurisdictions and individual courts have no resources to monitor vendor compliance and other centralized functions of program management.

Administrative interlock programs are appealing, at least in part, because of the challenge created when interlocks can by ordered by any one of hundreds of county court systems, in which only some of the judges are fully familiar with the provisions of the State's interlock laws. The number of courts and the independence of the judiciary render communicating on a large scale difficult, and achieving anything close to common practice nearly impossible, without active central coordination and court monitoring. In response to this problem, in August 2007, NHTSA convened a meeting of national leaders from the judicial community in an effort to open a dialogue about interlock programs.

Unlike the judiciary, State licensing authorities (usually departments of motor vehicles) are more hierarchical and have fewer people involved in making safety decisions. This renders the State agency a potentially more efficient means of increasing interlock-controlled driving. The licensing authority can withdraw the driving privilege from the DWI offender but, unlike the court system, has less leverage to alter driver behavior through other means. There is a risk with purely administrative programs that the most intransigent offenders will avoid enrollment in interlock programs and drive without a license and without insurance. In the context of administrative programs, requiring an interlock device as a path to full license reinstatement after a DWI conviction can result in interlock-controlled driving only if the offender is motivated to possess a valid license. It has been argued that administrative programs fail to control the most egregious offenders. In both Canada and Sweden, interlock programs are administrative. However, we lack a full understanding of how purely administrative programs propose to control the most difficult and resistant offenders when many in this category are so willing to drive without a license.

- **Internal Communication and Central Authority**
  In some States, there is judicial implementation (where the courts order and the probation department monitors the program), but a State authority oversees the operation of the interlock program. In several cases, comments suggest there may be too little interaction or coordination of resources, but there are exceptions when it seems to work well. When there is not a well established communications and coordination protocol, management of the program is sometimes haphazard. Much of this commentary was described earlier in the section on reporting.
  The Virginia program (managed by VASAP) has hybrid elements. By statute, it is administrative, but courts can add time to the sentences and courts are used to sanction noncompliant probationers. VASAP case managers review monthly reports. These case managers decide on appropriate action and can send offenders back to court if they so choose. New Mexico's program also incorporates both elements, including a judicial program for new convictions and an administrative program of interlock use for revoked offenders who want to drive during their revocation period. The New Mexico Department of Transportation Traffic Safety Bureau has oversight over all interlock providers and also manages the indigent fund.

There was a theme in the commentary provided by key informants in several States, suggesting that judges and prosecutors are ill informed about interlocks, what the devices do and how they should work. One provider concluded that the judiciary needs significant education about interlocks. Commentary from key informants suggests that this is a widespread problem and that many judges are not familiar with their State interlock laws. The NHTSA meeting in August 2007, was an attempt to elicit questions and improve information flow from judiciary opinion leaders.

In California, new legislation is under consideration, but at this writing, a judicial program is administered by the courts and a separate early reinstatement program is administered by DMV. Each program stands alone and operates concurrently, but the judicial program is the most prominent and judges decide who will have or who will avoid an interlock. In Florida, the program operates administratively, but judges can order the interlock as a condition of supervised probation. In Westchester County, New York, the interlock coordinator for the probation department suggested that the program would work most efficiently if there were probation officers who have interlock-specific caseloads. This would allow for a higher level of scrutiny and familiarity with the device and providers. This coordinator also favored (on interlock site) a review of records while meeting with clients, noting that communication between the provider and probation is the key to future referrals.

- **Recommendation: Information Sharing**

  With adequate resources, the State authority could both manage the interlock programs and mount efforts to educate the judiciary about how the interlock programs work in their State. Statewide protocols might help develop a higher level of communication between the administrative and judicial programs. The recent coordination role played by NHTSA could help facilitate a plan by which national justice leaders can broker better communication between State DMV and courts. If, for some reason, there is no formalized mechanism for exchanges between the courts and the State authority, then the provider should be required to supply that link so minimally acceptable types of information can pass between the two. If interlock companies provide services to the Government, then they have must provide information, as well. In States where there are sufficient numbers of offenders reporting to probation officers, it might be a worthwhile to consider a limited number of interlock experts within each local jurisdiction to manage the interlock cases, because understanding how to think about the interlock requirements is specialized information.

- **Alternative Methods for Courts to Document Abstinence**

  The philosophical issue raised throughout this report touches on the question of how an order to remain abstinent can coincide with an interlock program, especially one without concurrent treatment support structures. The courts have a tradition of imposing a standard of abstinence on DWI offenders and, currently, many are interested in using the interlock BAC test record to serve as an objective metric for attainment of that standard. The interlock is a vehicle sanction that records the BAC of someone starting the vehicle. Most interlock programs expect other family members to use the interlock vehicle. That is part of the interlock's appeal. It does not commandeer the vehicle, but shares the vehicle with other users or family members. So, how does the court know whether the offender under an abstinence order was responsible for one or more positive BAC tests recorded on the interlock shared by others? It cannot know. Some courts have solved the problem of "who blew" by making the offender responsible for all breath tests. A person's blood, urine and breath are unique to the individual; the vehicle is not. If that is the objective, it might be worthwhile for the courts to consider using other forms of monitoring that are unique to the convicted offender.

  Alcohol biomarkers (trace indicators of alcohol that can be measured days to weeks after drinking), or transdermal alcohol monitoring bracelets (such as SCRAM) have appeal because the results, unlike the log file from a vehicle interlock, can be explicitly linked to a single individual. Alternatively, one or more interlock companies now produce a device that is cost compatible with the interlock (approximately $2.25 per day), but that can test the individual at home (for example, the Smart Start interlock company produces a device called "InHom"; the Lifesafer interlock company has a similar type of device in development). The Smart Start device is identical to an interlock in some ways. The data is downloaded monthly at an interlock service center, costs the same as an interlock, but unlike most current interlocks, snaps a photo of the person providing the breath sample. Offenders would be expected to use the InHom two or more times every day. The device would link the photo to the breath test results and, over the course of 30 days, would provide a daily record (at whatever hourly interval desired) that the court could use to test adherence to the abstinence order.

Any of the above approaches to abstinence monitoring would be more specific alternatives to measuring abstinence compliance than an interlock device record. A topic that is discussed frequently is whether the interlock device *per se* should have features built into it that link a specific breath test to a specific driver. Establishing that the offender provided the breath samples (for sanctioning, extending, or rewarding) raises the question of whether it is important to have the identity of the driver (blower) established. Judges and prosecutors ordinarily support this idea and several interlock companies have undertaken efforts to photograph the driver/blower for this purpose. New technology from an overseas company appears capable of identifying the blower through face recognition technology, but as stated previously, this effort to identify the driver may be at odds with the purpose of the interlock and add unnecessary costs to interlock programs.

If an offender's interlock period is to be extended, however, it seems that crediting the breath-test results to the individual could be important. Some jurisdictions overcome this problem by informing the offender that he or she is responsible for all breath tests recorded on the interlock vehicle. One example of that directive occurred in Texas, where the court found that the offender was responsible for all breath tests. If such an order is sufficient, then positive identification may be superfluous, but it is unlikely to always be quite that straightforward. In the Texas case, the offender offered no evidence to suggest the offender was not the person who provided the sample. Without a challenge, it is not much of a court test. Whatever the result, the safety gain from positive identification should be evaluated against a possible safety loss that could follow from upward pressure on the cost of the interlock that narrows the pool of those who can afford to participate. Some additional costs should be expected as technology improves, but benefits should be relative to costs.

- **Recommendation: Alternative Methods for Monitoring Drinking**

  This topic of alternative BAC test measures was not explicitly discussed by the expert panel, but it is germane to the discussion and warrants consideration by courts that might desire a positive identification of offenders who are ordered to remain alcohol abstinent. Conceivably, the interlock BAC record can serve as a bridge technology until a time when more definitive and appropriate BAC monitoring methods are available more widely. Devices that are cost compatible with an interlock and can be specific to the individual offender should be considered seriously by courts that desire this form of alcohol control assurance.

7. Core Elements to Consider for Ignition Interlock Programs

The last topic of the expert panel meeting was devoted to commentary about which elements should be considered of key importance in designing an ideal interlock program. Although there was insufficient time to prioritize the key elements, and many topics were mentioned without the benefit of debate among all the seated experts, topics worthy of consideration did emerge and should be considered by State programs seeking to develop their own core program. Accordingly, these elements should not be viewed as either comprehensive or universally endorsed by all panelists. These are interesting and potentially useful features that reflect on the experience of panelists, but in many cases, were not discussed fully. Upon review of the topics, the following themes emerged: public understanding and deterrence, policy and program management, monitoring and reporting, issues for the judiciary and other issues. Many of these suggestions are compatible with or extensions of an earlier section in this report on Program Ramp Up.

This section ends with a brief review of the New Mexico program, since it is currently the only interlock program with a comprehensive analysis of its impact and a documented attainment of 50 percent installation of interlocks among convicted DWI offenders.

- **Public Understanding and Deterrence**
    1. Public understanding and outreach can provide important support to a newinterlock program; that is, the citizens should be engaged in the effort to make the roads safer from alcohol offenders.
    2. It was suggested that we promote the general deterrence effect of interlocks as a means to help build support for public buy-in.
    3. It was noted that general deterrence is achieved when an offender is issued an interlock license, whether or not the offender drives the interlock vehicle.
- **Policy and Management of the Program**

1. To overcome the temptation to drive while unlicensed, consequences of increasing severity should be applied. More targeted enforcement might help here, as would programs that require a period of interlock controlled driving prior to relicensing.
2. Solve the "no-vehicle" problem (offenders who claim to no longer own a vehicle and, therefore, do not warrant an interlock). How should we sanction, monitor, or incentivize offenders who assert no interest in driving? One suggestion is the use of alternative alcohol monitoring devices. Santa Fe County, New Mexico, attained a 71 percent installation rate among convicted DWI offenders when judges there required an electronic monitoring device as an alternative to the interlock. Any such approach would require that the judiciary be engaged.
3. A motivational counseling component or other treatment program, linked to the interlock record of breath tests, could help make interlock-stimulated changes in drinking more permanent.
4. Offenders who continue to blow positive BAC tests while using the interlock should be extended until they attain some period of alcohol-free driving (e.g., no BAC lockouts for 3 to 6 months).
5. Second offenders should use the interlock for a minimum of 2 years. It was also suggested that those who refuse BAC tests should use interlocks for longer periods of time.
6. It was suggested that third offenders use the interlock for 3 years or serve 10 years either on probation with the interlock required for half that time, using SCRAM (transdermal alcohol bracelet), or using another device to monitor drinking.
7. A general suggestion was made that 6 to 12 months be added for refusals or for an arrest BAC of .15+ g/dL.
8. There is a clear need for the establishment of reciprocity guidelines between jurisdictions with different interlock programs.
9. Regarding indigent funding, there is a need to have both a fund and an objective way to determine indigent status, so funds can be administered fairly. Currently, in New Mexico, judges often make determinations based on vague criteria. Criteria should be established and applied in a firm, defensible and standardized manner.

10. Can interlocks be installed on rental vehicles? This is not a core part of a program hierarchy, but worthy of consideration. How are rental companies handling this now? No answer was provided by panelists.
11. The interlock restriction MUST be noted on the license for the benefit of law enforcement officers and other authorities, including law enforcement from other States.
12. Vehicle forfeiture should be available as an option by the authorities when an offender is driving on a revoked license, because it is appropriate to impose a stronger sanction when a restriction is violated. However, it was noted in counterpoint that seizing and selling the vehicle is difficult when many vehicles may belong to persons other than the offenders. It was noted, however, that vehicle sanctions for DWI offenses can be difficult to support.
13. At the time of the panel discussion, it was stated that, in Illinois, it is possible to put an interlock on during hard suspension but the offender cannot drive. It was noted that this is difficult to implement and is similar to the issues highlighted in California and New Mexico in recent research by California's Department of Motor Vehicles (DeYoung et al., 2005; Roth, Voas, & Marques, 2007a).
14. The question was raised: Should there be an override option available? An override allows the locked-out offender to elect to bypass the interlock if he or she feels there is a pressing need that might be life threatening (e.g., exceptionally cold weather). The first example was in the Quebec program. Florida also has an override option. The pros and cons were discussed briefly. In all override programs, the vehicle enters a lockout once shutdown and use of this feature must be explained and justified. Research by Marques et al. (2003) determined that those offenders in Quebec who elected to use the bypass option were later found to be more likely to have significantly more subsequent DWI charges.
15. Regarding lockout set points, all except Florida are in the range of .02 to .03 in the United States; Alberta is .04; Florida at .051 is well above the NHTSA recommended set point of .025.
16. Interlock licensing, such as is available in New Mexico, should be expanded. With the interlock license, the driver's license remains

revoked officially, but if an interlock is installed and insurance acquired, it is a compromise that supports public safety (based on reduction in overall repeat DWI offenses for revoked offenders). This applies to most, but not all, DWI offenders (e.g., not offenders of vehicular homicide).

A question was raised regarding the requirement for minimum use of the interlock vehicle (e.g., to preclude parking it and waiting out the interlock requirement). Can there be a legal sanction for not using the vehicle? The answer was that it serves more as a way to bring in an offender for an administrative review session. According to most informants, this is used more often for reporting, rather than sanctioning for non-use of the vehicle. Of course, the motive for imposing this reporting requirement is because non-use of the interlock vehicle raises concern that an offender is using an alternative vehicle.

- **Monitoring and Reporting**
  1. Some form of monitoring is needed to ensure that the interlock requirement does not cause offenders to stop drinking alcohol and shift instead to another impairing substance, such as benzodiazepines.
  2. There is a clear need to monitor the vendors (service providers) actively, with at least one unannounced onsite visit per year.
  3. Standardized electronic reporting is very important and should be a high priority.
  4. Some kind of vehicle usage criteria are warranted, such as odometer checks, which are used in New Mexico, total run time or start frequency.
  5. Manufacturers should converge on a common set of recording protocols, so that alcohol content breath samples are recorded as the same events across all devices.
- **Issues for the Judiciary**
  1. There should be an effort to ensure judicial compliance with State law and some method of accountability instituted to encourage judges to follow State statute.
  2. Judges and prosecutors should have one or two standard alternatives for the "novehicle" problem (offenders who claim to no longer have a vehicle, will not drive and, therefore, do not warrant an interlock). An example of an alternative is an ankle

bracelet that monitors transdermal alcohol or a motion detector device that can detect driving.

3. First-offender programs are recommended, to have a more complete effect on public safety.
4. There should be a plan to anticipate and overcome the administrative burden, wherever it is; an example mentioned was magistrate courts that must deal with offenders, but have no probation capability. Courts that have probation authority should have the resources to ensure that someone is available to review monthly reports in order to monitor offenders.
5. There is a need for an effective way to react to judicial discretion that does not follow the law. For example, in Florida, the administrative program imposes the interlock requirement if judges do not. Texas now has a judicial liaison to mediate solutions to this issue. It was noted that prosecutors, not judges, “cutting deals” is often the source of the problem. A judicial liaison can help address problems of this kind.
6. The program should be concerned about “wet reckless” cases, because violations coded this way are a clear risk indicator. A wet reckless is a DWI arrest that is altered to reflect only a reckless driving charge. Colorado has a lesser offense, driving while ability impaired DWAI with BAC in the range of .05 to .079, that is a lesser offense than the standard DWI.
7. Many believe that hard suspension of a minimum period is advisable for general deterrence (30 to 45 days was suggested), but others prefer immediate interlock.
8. We should do more than educate just the judiciary. Education and training is necessary for all—prosecutors, probation, defense, court administrators, DMV personnel, treatment providers, law enforcement, legislators, court clerks, the public. Education about the public responsibility of the vendors is also recommended.
9. There should be procedures for immobilization of a vehicle or an interlock requirement before adjudication for repeat offenders. However, this will not work in a probation before judgment (PBJ) State.

- **Other Issues**
    1. The causes of interlock failures should be documented and, related to that, the urban legends about interlock shortcomings that are now historical anecdotes should be overcome with

current, accurate information. One suggestion was to establish a procedure, whereby interlock offenders may register a problem that can be investigated (to confirm or debunk faulty equipment claims). Presumably, this could be funded by the industry, but managed independently. This would serve as a useful counterpoint to unfounded claims, and to document legitimate problems.

2. It was suggested that any license, even a limited license, should not be granted without an interlock. Anyone with a DWI violation has earned an interlock.
3. Medical review—Maryland was the first State to establish a medical review board. Today, other States also have provisions for medical exceptions (e.g., Florida requires a review by a pulmonologist for exceptions related to blowing/breath capacity). It was suggested that, by altering flow rate, we can still get a rough estimate of levels. The current NHTSA Model Specifications require 1.5 L of air. It was noted that the new European standard for general public interlocks (not offender interlocks) requires only 0.7 L air.
4. What is the central purpose of interlock? To prevent impaired drivers from operating a vehicle. Should this be atop a hierarchy of program design and not become secondary to other objectives?
5. Is an abstinence-based program compatible with the purpose of an interlock? The program will work better if interlock is one component of a more comprehensive monitoring program scaled to driver risk.

- **New Mexico's Comprehensive Interlock Program**

  States interested in emulating a well thought through set of program features may want to study the development of the interlock program in New Mexico. As of 2008, the State of New Mexico has taken sustained efforts to enact a mutually supporting web of pragmatic laws, while closing loopholes left open by earlier provisions. Currently, in New Mexico, all convicted offenders are required to install interlocks. An interlock license can be obtained very soon after arrest if the offender can show proof of insurance (and did not commit a vehicular homicide). Past DWI offenders who are revoked can obtain an interlock license to allow interlock-controlled driving during their full revocation period. The State has established an indigent fund, which can pay up to half of the monthly fees for qualified offenders. The program is not perfect. New Mexico still lacks some pragmatic features. For example, it lacks monitoring for revoked offenders who obtain interlocks through the licensing act, it lacks intervention support services for those who are trying to embrace behavior change, it lacks a provision for extending offenders on the interlock until a criterion of zero BAC-positive lockouts are attained and it does not support an alternative alcohol-monitoring requirement that can be used with those who succeed in avoiding an interlock by claiming to have no vehicle and no intention to drive. The New Mexico legislature continues to consider bills that close existing loopholes and attempt to further improve the laws in an effort to place all DWI offenders onto an interlock program. By 2005, the State had enacted six laws pertaining to the operation of its interlock program. The New Mexico laws include both administrative and judicial components.*

The New Mexico laws and program have resulted in significant increases in interlock use. Moreover, the State has experienced reductions in alcohol crashes, alcohol crash injuries and alcohol fatalities. These reductions can not necessarily be attributed exclusively to New Mexico's ignition interlock program, since a number of other important initiatives designed to reduce impaired driving have also been underway during the same period of time. However, these State trends are promising. Research has been conducted by the State and Robert Wood Johnson's Substance Abuse Policy Research Program. Research papers can be found in the peer reviewed literature and a comprehensive evaluation of the New Mexico program is undergoing agency review at NHTSA (Marques et al.; not yet published).

Interview comments suggest that, even in New Mexico, there are still judges who suffer from a lack of current information about interlocks; there are reports of poor information flow in some cases between courts and providers; and there are other sub-optimal conditions for maximizing the safety benefits of these instruments. Several counties in the State have very low installation rates; by contrast, Santa Fe County had attained a 71 percent rate in 2003-2005 (Roth et al., 2009). Discussions with judges and prosecutors in low-income counties suggest that economic hardship is a major deterrent for them.

- **Recommendation: The New Mexico Program Is a Good Place to Start**

New Mexico has the most well-developed interlock laws and the best evaluation information. It is far from perfect, but at the intersection of evidence and effort, it is a good place for interlock programs to start to gain insight, especially for those States that are just getting started or planning to upgrade their features.

8. Miscellaneous Other Topics

There are many more considerations that could be cited beyond those mentioned previously. This report does not propose a program standard, but rather provides a spectrum of recommendations for consideration. Other topics are worthy of consideration as well, if only because they affect large portions of the country (rural programs) and numbers of road users (motorcycles). Some features are worth considering because they have already been used in some U.S. jurisdictions and in Canada (emergency overrides). Some topics are mentioned here as well, but are more properly in the province of device certification guidelines.

- **Rural Interlock Programs**
  Blatt and Furman (1998) reported that most crashes occur on rural roads and that the crashes disproportionately involve rural residents. Their data showed also that young rural drivers are at the greatest risk. Considering the high involvement of young people in alcohol crashes, it may be that there is a significant need for interlock programs in rural areas. Marques, Tippetts, and Voas (2004) examined interlock records by postal code to study whether rural residence in Alberta and Quebec, Canada, was a factor in alcoholrelated road risks and could find no greater (or lesser) alcohol lockout rates in rural drivers. However, it is clear that, since interlocks are deemed to be a good safety intervention for urban and suburban motorists, they should be available as a safety option for rural residents as well. However, managing rural programs is not always straightforward since dedicated interlock services centers are rarely sustainable economically in thinly populated areas. In States with large rural areas, interlock service centers can be a long drive for most residents. Some interlock vendors have used mobile vans for servicing interlocks; others have developed a mail-back interlock that an offender can swap out and return to the company monthly. Others, contract with suppliers of aftermarket automotive products to provide interlock services.

- **Recommendation: Rural Programs**
  There are no specific recommendations from the expert panel, but there are a variety of experiences from the field. For example, the large number of interlock service providers in New Mexico formed a loose alliance, so each would have some responsibility for providing rural service while also having some arrangement that allowed for sharing of the more lucrative urban markets.

- **Emergency Override**
  The question was raised: Should there be an override option available for emergencies? An override allows the locked-out offender to elect to bypass the interlock if he or she feels there is a pressing need that might be life threatening (e.g., exceptionally cold weather). In all override programs described, the vehicle enters a lockout once the engine is shut down and use of this feature must be explained and justified. The first example was in the Canadian program. Florida has since adopted an override option. In jurisdictions that have adopted this option, selection of the override option sets lights flashing and horn blaring to warn other motorists to stay clear.
  Canada and several States have allowed an override option (if a manufacturer's device supports it). Some States provide for a fail-safe option, such that an interlock can be overridden but, if used, must be brought immediately to the service facility. In Maryland, the option is available in rare and extreme emergency situations and the *vendor* may authorize the driver to override the device. The device locks out within 24 hours if not reset at the service center. It is not clear if the override is permitted by a State only if certain devices have an override capability built in or whether it is actively requested as a feature by the State. Most States have no override provision.
  - **Recommendation: Emergency Override**
    In the panel meeting, there was some support for this from a few participants, but no endorsement by most. This option was first adopted in the late 1990s in Quebec, Canada. Evaluation of the Quebec data (Marques et al., 2003) showed there was a higher likelihood of using the override by offenders had higher rates of elevated BAC tests. Later post-interlock recidivism evidence showed that those who used the override more were significantly more likely to have post-interlock repeat DWI charges. It was a weak effect, and it may not mean anything other than people with higher levels of BAC are more apt to need the override if they

could not start the vehicle. There may be a valid argument that an override could be beneficial if controlled by the provider or by the State authority if it was a one use option that would result in lockout shortly after the vehicle engine is shutdown. In Quebec as in Florida, use of this option was discouraged by activation of lights and horn while driving. Jurisdictions considering this feature should contact officials in jurisdictions that have used it. Override continues to be an optional feature in Canada.

- **Early Release**
  In the panel discussion, some commentary was directed not just toward using the interlock event record as a basis for adding further time or sanctions, but also as a means of rewarding those who are compliant. Not all panelists liked the idea and a counterpoint was suggested that, before considering the reduction of sentences, more information from independent risk estimates is warranted. In jurisdictions with active teams of probation officers, alternative sources of information may be attainable. Most likely would prefer some *objective* form of secondary evidence. One such type is any of several blood or urine biomarkers that reflect past alcohol use and can serve as indicators of continued drinking (Marques et al., 2009). These, of course, introduce additional costs, but if biomarkers were used selectively on problem cases, then costs could be controlled.
  - **Recommendation: Early Release From the Interlock Program**
    There are several ways to determine, through use of urine or blood tests, whether alcohol consumption has been brought under control. While alcohol itself is cleared from circulation within several hours of drinking, alcohol biomarkers can be found for many days after a drinking episode. Programs considering early release from an interlock obligation should acquire supplemental sources of information to assure that the offender has not just been avoiding use of the interlock vehicle. If drinking genuinely has been brought under control, then public risk exposure will have been reduced, making early release defensible.
- **Motorcycle Interlocks**
  Before motorcycle interlocks can be considered in an interlock program, there would need to be a motorcycle-specific device available for certification testing. Interlocks are being installed in motorcycles, but not very many since some of the manufacturers have liability concerns. Motorcycle interlocks could not operate in the same

way as vehicle interlocks do, without becoming a safety hazard (e.g., running retest requirements would have to be satisfied only after pulling over to the side of the road). We had no reports of motorcycle interlocks having been devised that meet their own certification standards, and they currently are not covered by the NHTSA Model Specifications. There is no reason that a State could not write a specification for devices to guide manufacturers' development. But some manufacturers have commented that there is no business model that warrants the investment needed for developing new devices.

- **Recommendation: Motorcycle Interlocks**
  There is no recommendation on this topic. It seems reasonable to consider a motorcycle interlock, but it also seems that, for safety sake, a motorcycle device would need different certification guidelines and testing protocols, such as allowing retests only when speed had dropped to zero.

- **Calibration Intervals**
  This is one of the topics that cuts across the device and program standards. The NHTSA (1992) Model Specifications currently call for service intervals between 30 to 60 days. Most States accept the interlock provider recommendations, which are based on the 1992 NHTSA Model Specifications.
  - **Recommendation: Calibration Intervals**
    In the earliest days of interlock programs, devices were subject to considerable calibration drift and required at least bimonthly service visits. The strongest motive for frequent service checking now appears to be compliance related because modern equipment is inherently more stable. A related benefit to regular service calls is the opportunity to talk with the customer/offender. If there were a separate program element that addressed treatment or counseling issues, as distinct from the interlock device, and if the interlock record could be downloaded remotely for review, then this could present an opportunity to shift costs for device monitoring over to offender monitoring and/or rehabilitation. Reduced frequency of visits based on performance also might serve as an incentive for good behavior. However the inter-service intervals may be determined, the basis should serve safety; not following tradition for its own sake.

- **Retest Failure or Retest Refusal**
  With a few exceptions, lockout set points in North America are in the range of .02 to .03.; Two exceptions are Alberta, Canada at .04 and Florida, which locks out at .051.
  Failure to retest (i.e., while the engine is running and a retest requirement is signaled by the interlock) is seen as a serious violation in many States, but there is variation in what the consequences are for ignoring a retest request. Some States require activation of an immediate signal, such as the horn, lights or a siren (in Colorado), when refusal occurs. A key informant in Pennsylvania noted that there can be no audible tone issued following this class of violations since such vehicle sounds are against Pennsylvania Vehicle Code law. In Pennsylvania, there is no separate penalty for failing to submit to or pass a rolling retest, except that the offender has to pay a service fee to have the interlock reset (e.g., the cost in this case is inconvenience and money rather than other penalties). In Maryland, failure to submit to rolling retests is a violation that is reported to the MVA and probation, but it does not disable the vehicle. In New Mexico, retest failure results in horn activation until the vehicle is turned off. Then, a 3-minute delay occurs before the restart option is available. Retest delay intervals seem to be set by the hardware provided by vendor and generally are not established by State statute. States vary greatly. Also, if there is to be an audible signal to alert outsiders to the violation, informants recommended that it be *unique.*_The horn was found, in at least one State, to result in physical confrontation with other drivers who thought the beeping horn was intentional or rude hurrying. Following a retest refusal in California, the LED lights will display "LOCK" for 48 hours, after which it will lockout.
  - **Recommendation: Lockout and Retest Refusal**
    Since the specifications for lockout BAC are device-related, the new NHTSA interlock device standard might specify how the interlock itself responds to retest failures/ refusals. Nonetheless, all these events must be recorded in the log file. However, States should discuss this issue and review pros and cons. It is difficult to know from the responses received what common view would be best, and the expert panel did not address this issue. Presumably, one or two retest refusals prior to an engine shutdown would be less significant (e.g., the driver had arrived at his/her destination just as the retest was requested) than repeated

retest refusals while underway, and certainly less significant than retest failures. This is one of many issues that will be dependent on States to devise innovative methods to manage its interlock offenders.

CONCLUSION

This document represents the authors' interpretation of evidence from a variety of sources including a compilation of key informant survey results and subsequent discussions during the expert panel meeting. All panelists who participated in the session received a copy of the first draft of this report and were asked to provide review and comment.

It appears that interlock programs in the United States may develop along two different tracks to accommodate the widely differing views on how the devices should be used. The two primary configurations seem to vary based on the evidence of risk and the involvement of the court system in managing that risk. As experience with interlock programs grows, there may come a time when the interlock program features can be selected more thoughtfully based on objective evidence of offender risk and the best approach to intervention to attain reductions in both individual and public risk exposure. Currently, the research basis for selecting program features is thin. A research plan that investigates the public benefit of different program features is overdue and could help settle differences of opinion with evidence.

Conceivably, the best way to structure interlock programs is to impose on offenders a level of monitoring and restriction that matches the level of public risk that they represent. When the Farr-Davis Driver Safety Act in California was passed in 1986, there was no basis for configuring the programs. No one knew enough then, or for many years after, how to devise the best program structures. In the absence of any clear guidelines, States developed a variety of approaches to the use of alcohol interlock devices. These efforts have yielded the imperfect systems that we must sift through today to make recommendations about the most promising ways to proceed with interlock programs. Often, the program structures that have been put in place reflect differing philosophies, none of which are all right or all wrong; few have been evaluated. As a result, no single program is known to have satisfactorily addressed all implementation and control problems.

The expert panel advised that pragmatic approaches are more defensible than punitive approaches. Pragmatism favors reducing the risk of alcohol crashes above all other considerations and, according to the foundational statement: first protect the public. For DWI offenders, we believe the evidence at this stage suggests we should install the interlocks early, use them until there is evidence of behavior change, actively monitor both offender and vendor performance during the interlock program and heavily ramp-up enforcement to ensure that driving while suspended does not become a preferred low-risk alternative to the interlock for DWI offenders. Those offenders who are supposed to be driving under the control of an interlock and are not – or who are suspended/revoked from drinking and driving – should be subject to a more restrictive level of behavior control, such as monitoring bracelets. Relative to wearing a monitoring bracelet on the ankle, the interlock on the vehicle will be a cheaper and more appealing alternative. Unfortunately, there is insufficient evidence to solidly embrace this pragmatic approach, just as there is insufficient evidence to show the pragmatic approach is not exactly the best way to deal with the DWI problem.

Among the States that have seen promise in interlock programs as a path to safer roads, the State of New Mexico, due to an unusual intersection of political will and personal experiences of legislators from both political parties, has made more effort than other States (as of 2008) to enact a mutually supporting web of pragmatic laws, while closing loopholes left open by earlier provisions. Currently, all convicted offenders are required to install interlocks, the interlock should be available for installation very soon after arrest, past DWI offenders whose licenses are revoked can obtain an interlock license to drive during their revocation period (provided they show proof of insurance and did not commit a vehicular homicide) and an indigent fund pays up to half of the monthly fees for qualified offenders. New Mexico still lacks some pragmatic features. For example, it lacks monitoring for revoked offenders who obtain interlocks through the licensing act, it lacks intervention support services for those who are trying to embrace behavior change, it lacks a provision for extending offenders on the interlock until zero BAC positive lockouts are attained and it lacks an alternative alcohol-monitoring requirement that can be used with those who claim no vehicle and no intention to drive. The New Mexico legislature continues to consider bills that close existing loopholes as it attempts to further improve the laws in an effort to place all DWI offenders onto an interlock program. By 2005, the State had enacted six laws pertaining to the operation of its interlock program. The New Mexico laws include both administrative and judicial components. New bills are introduced during each legislative session.

The New Mexico laws and program have resulted in significant increases in interlock use, attaining an installation rate of 50 percent of all DWI convictions, which is vastly more than other States. Moreover, no other State has documented its interlock program as carefully as has New Mexico, and the State has experienced reductions in alcohol crashes, alcohol crash injuries and alcohol fatalities.

These reductions can not necessarily all be attributed to New Mexico's ignition interlock program, since a number of other important initiatives designed to reduce impaired driving have also been underway during the same period of time. However, these State trends are promising.

Even in New Mexico, there are still judges who suffer from a lack of current information about the interlock; there are reports of poor information flow in some cases between courts and providers; there is inconsistent use of the indigent fund and there are other sub-optimal conditions for maximizing the safety benefit of these instruments. Several counties in the State have very low installation rates. Discussions with judges and prosecutors in low-income counties suggest that economic hardship is a major deterrent for them.

New Mexico has a good base. It lacks several features (as detailed above) that could be important elements in a model comprehensive interlock program. An eclectic program that uses many of the features from New Mexico and selected features from other States may be best of all. However, any program that is based primarily on a judicial model will need to develop better methods of communicating with judges and prosecutors. In the near term, an administrative program core that has good judicial communication and solid judicial support might attain quicker success. In this respect, the program in Florida may provide the basis for a good administrative program model with hybrid elements because it is mandatory (for re-licensure), it is statewide, it has judicial support, and it is being actively researched. The question for the Florida program is whether it can lead to the installation of interlocks on more vehicles of DWI offenders without reducing the number of offenders who opt to drive without a license. Time will tell. After this project began to identify key features of interlock programs, new mandatory State interlock laws covering all offenders were enacted in several States, including Arizona, Washington and Louisiana.

Recidivism rates, alcohol crashes and alcohol fatalities ultimately will provide the kind of data we need to judge the success and adequacy of statewide programs.

APPENDIX A. ICADTS-IWG SURVEY QUESTIONS

Questions developed by PIRE and the ICADTS Interlock Working Group for Key Informants based on discussions at the 7th Ignition Interlock Symposium, Beaver Creek, Colorado, October 2006.

Monitoring Offenders

How are offenders monitored for program compliance/violations, by whom?
Are monthly reports provided by the interlock service company on each offender? Who acts upon them? Where are they sent?
What is in the reports and how frequently are they generated? Are they paper or electronic?
What action does your State or jurisdiction take upon receiving violation reports? If no action, why?

Offender Requirements

Interlock required on one vehicle or all?
Is there a hard suspension period before interlock can be used? How long? first offenders, 2nd offenders, 3rd + offenders
Can offenders avoid interlock by waiting out full suspension period until eligible for re-licensure?
Are there restrictions on when and where interlock users can drive?
Is there a minimum required amount of vehicle use every month? If yes, how is this checked (odometer, start up tests, other)?
Is interlock offered as an alternative to suspension under the ALR law either from the date of arrest or after a period of hard suspension?
To prevent use of the vehicle between arrest and interlock installation, does your program provide for: …license plate seizure? …vehicle impoundment? …immobilization?…other?
Violations & Penalties
At what BAC does the interlock prevent a start in your jurisdiction? Are there different levels for different types of offenders (e.g., drivers under 21)?
If an elevated BAC test locks out the ignition successfully and prevents a start up, is that considered a program violation? What are the penalties?
What are penalties for violations such as tampering and circumvention (e.g., fines, increased suspension, longer interlock time, removal from program, jail)?
Do you find circumvention efforts are rare, occasional or common?

What is the most typical methods used?
Is a breath test override option available to bypass the interlock in case of emergency?
If yes, what outward signal (e.g., horn blowing, lights flashing, silent signal to authorities) shows an override has occurred? What about for a failure to take a rolling retest?
Does failure to provide a running retest result in lockout? How does that work?
Should the duration of the interlock sentence be dependent on performance? For example, should drivers' required interlock period be extended for failed start up attempts during the last 3 months before re-licensure? If yes, how many is too many? What is the best way to prevent circumvention at start up?
Do you think any offenders are using compressed air to start their interlock cars in your area?
Monitoring Providers
How are interlock providers monitored for compliance with State requirements? How often?
How are inspections conducted? Are unannounced inspections or pseudo-clients used (i.e., phony clients who are really inspectors)?
What is inspected? (accuracy of equipment, hum tone or suck/blow activated, etc.)?
What are penalties for lack of compliance, poor service? Are providers ever sanctioned by telling them they cannot do business in your area?
Does the interlock allow positive identification of the person who blows the BAC test (e.g., record photo of blower)?

Provider/Vendor Requirements

Does your State require fuel-cells as opposed to the semiconductor sensors?
Does the State specify that no feature of the device may be modified by the service company without approval from the State or regional authority?
Does the State specify that providers provide training for new interlock users? How much?
What is the maximum allowable length between interlock service inspections?
Does the length between inspections depend on offender behavior (e.g., less frequent for good behavior)?

Operation

Is the program judicial, administrative or have elements of both?
How is the program managed at the State or jurisdictional authority level?
Is there a single agency within the jurisdiction that oversees the program? What agency?
What role do prosecutors and judges play in the program?
What role do probation officers have?
Is there a single service company/vendor operating or several companies?
Do the service providers handle interlocks as a side business or solely as an interlock business? What led to adoption of this system?

Costs

Who pays for the program (e.g., government agencies, only the offenders, combination)? If the government contributes, where do funds come from (e.g., fines)?
How much does it cost per month?
Is there an indigent fund to help poorer people?

Associated Services

Are any of the interlock services linked to treatment programs? If so, is the treatment guided at all by contents of interlock data (e.g., positive samples)? Please describe the programs.
Are any of the interlock services operating in conjunction with a medical review program? Describe the program.
Is the program linked to a program such as DWI or drug courts? If so, please describe the program.
Are other devices or monitoring methods used in conjunction with the interlock (e.g., SCRAM, Sobrietor, alcohol biomarkers)? If so, describe the programs.
How does the offender get the car serviced for repairs that require mechanics to start and run the car?

Three More Questions

Have there been benefits to the implementation of your interlock program? What are they?
Have there been any problems which haven't been discussed yet?
Are there any other issues you would like to address which haven't been raised in this survey?

APPENDIX B. EXPERT PANEL

James Angelino
Defense Attorney
Former Denton Co. Prosecutor
2517 Cedar Elm Lane
Plano, TX 75075
jamesangelino@tx.rr.com

Jim Fell
Director, Traffic Safety &
Enforcement Programs Pacific
Institute for Research and Evaluation
11720 Beltsville Drive, Ste 900
Calverton, MD 20705-3166
Fell@pire.org

Doug Beirness, Ph.D.
Manager, Research & Policy
Canadian Centre for Substance
Abuse
75 Albert Street, Suite 300
Ottawa, Ontario K1P 5E7
CANADA
dougbeir@magma.ca

Hon. Tom Fuller
Criminal Court Judge at Law #5
Frank Crowley Courts Bldg.
133 N. Industrial Blvd. 3rd Floor
Dallas, TX 75207
judgefuller@earthlink.net

Donna Bevacqua-Young
Traffic Safety Resource Prosecutor
Administrative Office of the
District Attorneys
P.O. Box 6667
Santa Fe, NM 87502
dbevacqua@da.nm.state.us

Terry Gorman
Probation Officer
Westchester County Probation
Department
121 E. Post Rd. 3rd Floor
White Plains, NY 10601
Ttg5@westchestergov.com

David Bolyard
Director, Driver Services
West Virginia DMV
1800 Kanawha Blvd.
Charleston, WV 25317
dbevacqua@da.nm.state.us

Hon. Daryl R. Coffey
County Criminal Court #8
Tarrant County Justice Center
401 W. Belknap
Fort Worth, TX 76196-0401
dcoffey@tarrantcounty.com

Debra Coffey
Director of Judicial Services
Smart Start Inc.
4850 Plaza Drive
Irving, TX 75063
dcoffey@smartstartinc.com

James F. Frank, Ph.D.
Consultant, Monitech, Inc.
9216 Watson Road
Silver Spring, MD 20910-4136
jim.frank1@verizon.net

Paul R. Marques, Ph.D.
Project Director, Host
Senior Research Scientist
Pacific Institute
11720 Beltsville Drive, Ste 900
Calverton, MD 20705-3166
marques@pire.org

Hon. Karl B. Grube
Senior Judge
ABA/NHTSA Judicial Outreach
Liaison
P.O. Box 10354
St. Petersburg, FL 33733-0354
kgrube@jud6.org

Chuck Hurley
Chief Executive Officer
Mothers Against Drunk Driving
511 E. John Carpenter Freeway
Irving, TX 75062
Chuck.hurley@madd.org

Hon. Cristina Jaramillo
Albuquerque Metro Court Judge
Division III Court
P.O. Box 133,
Albuquerque, NM 87103-0133
DCastillo@metrocourt.state.nm.us

Barbara Lauer, Chief
Driver Education and DUI Programs
FL Dept Highway Safety & Motor
Vehicles,
Tallahassee, FL 32399-0571
Lauer.barbara@hsmv.state.fl.us

Carl A. Soderstrom, M.D.
Chief, Medical Advisory Board
Maryland Motor Vehicle
Administration
6601 Ritchie Highway, NE. - Room
47C
Glen Burnie, MD 21062
csoderstrom@mdot.state.md.us

Ian R. Marples, LL.B.
General Counsel
Alcohol Countermeasure Systems Corp
60 International Blvd.
Toronto, Ontario M9W 6J2, CANADA
imarples@acs-corp.com

Michael McConnell
Director, Interlock Quality Assurance Program
PA DUI Association
2413 N. Front Street
Harrisburg, PA 17110
mmcconnell@padui.org

Rob Mitchell
Administrator, Alternative Sentencing Division
San Juan County
1006 Municipal Dr.
Farmington, NM 87401
rmitchell@sjcounty.net

Tom Nochajski, Ph.D.
Professor, School of Social Work
University of Buffalo SUNY
660 Baldy Hall
Amherst, NY 14260
thn@buffalo.edu

William Rauch, Ph.D.
Center for Studies on Alcohol
Westat, Inc.
1650 Research Blvd.
Rockville, MD 20850
billrauch@westat.com

David Timken, Ph.D.
Center for Impaired Driving Research and Evaluation (CIDRE)
3153 Fern Pl.
Boulder, CO 80304
cidre@comcast.net

Richard Roth, Ph.D.
President, Impact DWI
2300 West Alameda Unit D4
Santa Fe, NM 87507
Richardroth2300@msn.com

Robert B. Voas, Ph.D.
Project Co-Director, Host
Senior Research Scientist
Pacific Institute for Research and Evaluation
11720 Beltsville Drive, Ste 900
Calverton, MD 20705-3166
voas@pire.org

NHTSA Participants:

Heidi L. Coleman, J.D.
Chief, Impaired Driving Division, NHTSA
1200 New Jersey Avenue SE.
Washington, DC 20590
Heidi.Coleman@dot.gov

Nancy Ross, J.D.
Highway Safety Specialist,
Impaired Driving Division, NHTSA
1200 New Jersey Avenue SE.
Washington, DC 20590
Nancy.Ross@dot.gov

Michael Sandoval
Chief, New Mexico Traffic Safety Bureau
604 W. San Mateo
Santa Fe, NM 87505
Michael.Sandoval@state.nm.us

Jeff Michael, Ed.D
Director
Office of Impaired Driving & Occupant Protection, NHTSA
1200 New Jersey Avenue SE.
Washington, DC 20590
Jeff.Michael@dot.gov

APPENDIX C. NON-U.S. INTERLOCK PROGRAM FEATURES

Swedish Program

In the Swedish interlock program, the largest component is a primary prevention interlock that is required on commercial vehicles (e.g., this aspect of the Swedish Alcolock Program is not an offender program, but an emerging requirement for all commercial vehicles). The offender program is different. Offenders are monitored via regular medical checkups and through the review of recorded BAC data logs every 3 months. The majority of interlocks installed in Sweden are in commercial vehicles.

In the offender program, if there are missed medical checks or elevated BAC tests, the County Council removes offenders from the program. This is one of those policy choices that might be counterproductive, since it could result in having the most alcohol dependent offenders unmonitored. The three national government representatives (from the Swedish National Road Administration) who commented on this question in the ICADTS-IWG survey felt it is better to maintain someone on the interlock and just extend the interlock time until 12 months of clean record are produced. However, the legislative support is not there yet. This policy divide is one that recurs in the United States, depending on the States involved, and is a good example of the difference between the public health/safety approach and the punitive approach. An interlock left on the vehicle at least has the benefit of reducing exposure to alcohol impaired drivers when that car is used, whereas an unlicensed or revoked driver still can choose to drive without an interlock. However, there are cultural differences and, reportedly, the likelihood of unlicensed driving is somewhat rarer in Sweden than it is in the United States or Canada.

The Swedish program does not require hard suspension prior to the interlock, as the interlock component is completely separate from the punishment component. The interlock in Sweden is configured as a component of an abstinence program. While an offender in Sweden can wait out the interlock (not elect to participate in the interlock program), the offender still must demonstrate non-dependency on alcohol and drugs before relicensure. (This is possible in Sweden, since they require the use of alcohol biomarker blood tests to assure minimal use of alcohol.) With the interlock, the offender can drive only inside Sweden and no minimum amount of driving is required. The consequence of blocked starts due to positive BAC is strict; if more than one elevated BAC test is found in a bimonthly report, then the person is dismissed from the program. All tampering and circumvention violations also result in dismissal, but again the respondents from the National Road Administration feel the offenders should be extended, rather than dismissed. Running retest failures or refusals result in horns blowing.

The Swedish device certification requires breath tests with air temperature and humidity requirements in a physiological range plus voice and/or inhalation requirements to assure valid tests. They have no provision for monitoring providers, but feel there should be some evaluation on the adequacy of the education that is provided to the clients. In this case, they suggest there should be an independent authority that checks on the installation facilities. The program in Sweden is administrative and it is managed by the County Council in each national region. There is no judicial role. Service providers currently have interlock as a sole business, but as the program accepts new vendors, it will include a mix of other types of businesses. The cost to the offender is approximately $300 USD per month, and this includes the interlock as well as the medical checks every 3 months. (These medical checks are the major cost item.) While the medical program requires alcohol biomarker analysis every 3 months, the program does not have an alcohol rehabilitation component – that is up to the offender – but the survey respondents believed it would be best if the rehabilitation component was integrated. They recognize vehicle repair bypass as a problem, but do not describe their approach. Also, they call for a standard interface between the car and device for all manufacturers.

Western Australian Program

This program has been the subject of much discussion at interlock symposia in 2004 to 2007, because it was built nearly entirely from evidence reported at meetings, shepherded through Parliament and divisions of government and has gained endorsement by the collective judgment of those who research and manage interlock programs. After passing the Parliament, the law hit a new roadblock in 2007, and still has not been implemented.

If it ever gets started, the program is expected to work well and there are likely to be fewer legislative fixes needed later. Monthly summary reports have been arranged to be sent to the traffic department with a highlight of violations. The latter will be acted upon immediately against standardized criteria, established under the authority of the director general of the Transport Department. Interlocks will be required on all vehicles owned. High-BAC first offenders and multiple offenders can elect to participate for reinstatement. The required minimal period of interlock is 6 months, but the condition will not be lifted until the record indicates successful separation of drinking and driving; that is, offenders will be extended on interlock for BAC lockouts. Offenders must have a period of interlock before full re-licensure. The interlock offender must bring the vehicle in for inspection. There is no restriction on driving and anyone can apply for an interlock license immediately after conviction. Since Australia has a vigorous program of random breath testing, drivers are stopped often and asked for BAC samples. The law allows for immediate roadside vehicle impoundment for 28 days for any offender without a valid license.

The basic lockout point is .02, but if someone registers three BACs of .05 g/dL or higher, that person must attend alcohol treatment and the interlock condition cannot be lifted until treatment is completed. A minimum of 6 months clean time is required before the interlock will be removed. Failed rolling retests result in hazard flashers and a siren that continues until the vehicle is stopped, plus a temporary lockout. The program does not include a provision for photo ID of the driver, but it does require that there be no modification of devices. The maximum allowable interval between device services is just 30 days. The program is fully administrative. It is overseen by the Licensing Department, but components are handled by the Justice Department (license disqualification and fines) and the Health Department (alcohol assessment and treatment). Prosecutors and judges play no role. Vendors handle interlocks and other products and services. Costs are split, with both the offender and government paying a portion. Government contributions come from drink driving fees. Early participants have their fines deferred and waived upon successful completion. The Western Australia government pays for alcohol assessment and treatment. The cost per month per participant is $150 AUS (~$125 US). There is also a health subsidy of $50 for those who have a Health Care Card; plus, an indigent fund will be established. This program was expected to commence on July 1, 2007, but it has been delayed. Interlocks have had a difficult time gaining traction in Australia. The State of Victoria, however, appears to have established a brisk and effective program with several thousand interlocks in service.

Canada Program Guidelines

The development of interlock programs in the United States and Canada have moved forward in concert with each other, beginning around 1990. It is fitting that, concurrent with the effort in the United States to identify program features, Doug Beirness of the Canadian Center for Substance Abuse in Ottawa has set upon a similar effort to suggest principles and core elements for national guidelines there. The following outline summarizes the topical features of the Canadian approach, as recently presented by Beirness at the 8th Ignition Interlock Symposium Meeting in 2007. All Canadian programs are administrative in nature. Some, like Alberta's, have quasi-judicial features.

Guiding Principles

- Incapacitation, not punishment or treatment
- Include all offenders
- Flexibility
- Breath test failures are not program failures
- Coordinated with other programs

Core Elements

- Legislation
- Program authority
- Technical standards
- Circumvention protection
- Threshold BAC
- Eligibility
- Early entry
- Program duration
- Criterion-based removal
- Notation on driver's license
- Monitoring
- Sanctions for violations
- Service providers

- Reporting
- Reciprocity

Optional Features

- Emergency override
- Pre-conviction participation
- Multiple short-term suspensions
- Early release

REFERENCES

Blatt, J. & Furman, S. M. (1998). Residence location of drivers involved in fatal crashes. *Accident Analysis and Prevention*, *30*(6), 705-711.

Coben, J. H. & Larkin, G. L. (1999). Effectiveness of ignition interlock devices in reducing drunk driving recidivism. *American Journal of Preventive Medicine*, *16*(1S), 81-87.

DeYoung, D. J., Tashima, H. N. & Maston, S. V. (2005). An evaluation of the effectiveness of ignition interlock in California. In P. R. Marques (Ed.), *Alcohol Ignition Interlock Devices—Volume II: Research, Policy, and Program Status 2005* (42-52). Oosterhout, The Netherlands: International Council on Alcohol, Drugs and Traffic Safety.

EMT Group (1990). Evaluation of the California ignition interlock pilot program for DUI offenders (Farr-Davis Driver Safety Act of 1986). California Office of Traffic Safety.

FBI. Crime in the United States, 2007. Uniform Crime Reports. Washington, DC: Federal Bureau of Investigation. Accessed at: http://www.fbi.gov/ucr/ucr.htm.

Marques, P. R., Tippetts, A. S., Allen, J., Javors, M., Alling, C., Yegles, M., et al. (2009, in press). Estimating driver risk using alcohol biomarkers, interlock BAC tests, and psychometric assessments: Initial descriptives. *Addiction*.

Marques, P. R., Tippetts, A. S. & Voas, R. B. (2003a). The Alcohol Interlock: An underutilized resource for predicting and controlling drunk drivers. *Traffic Injury Prevention*, *4*(3), 188194.

Marques, P. R., Tippetts, A. S. & Voas, R. B. (2003b). Comparative and joint prediction of DUI recidivism from alcohol ignition interlock and driver records. *Journal of Studies on Alcohol*, *64*(1), 83-92.

Marques, P. R., Tippetts, A. S. & Voas, R. B. (2004). Do rural drivers pose greater alcohol impaired driving risks? Driver record, questionnaire, and interlock BAC data as proxies for risk. In J. Oliver, P. Williams & A. Clayton (Eds.), *Proceedings of the 17th International Conference on Alcohol, Drugs and Traffic Safety, August 8-13, 2004*. Glasgow, UK: X-CD Technologies.

Marques, P. R., Tippetts, A. S., Voas, R. B. & Beirness, D. J. (2001). Predicting repeat DUI offenses with the alcohol interlock recorder. *Accident Analysis and Prevention*, *33*(5), 609619.

Marques, P. R., Voas, R. B., Roth, R. & Tippetts, A. S. (2009, in press). *Evaluation of the New Mexico Ignition Interlock Program.* Washington, DC: National Highway Traffic Safety Administration.

Marques, P. R., Voas, R. B. & Tippetts, A. S. (2003). Behavioral measures of drinking: Patterns in the interlock record. *Addiction*, *98*(Suppl 2), 13-19.

Marques, P. R., Voas, R. B., Tippetts, A. S. & Beirness, D. J. (1999). Behavioral monitoring of DUI offenders with the alcohol ignition interlock recorder. *Addiction*, *94*(12), 18611870.

Miller T. R. &Levy, D. T. (2000) Cost-outcome analysis in injury prevention and control: Eighty-Four recent estimates for the United States, *38* (6), 562-582.

McCartt, A., Wells, J. & Teoh, E. (2009). Attitudes toward in-vehicle advanced alcohol detection technology. Arlington, VA: Insurance Institute for Highway Safety.

McKnight, A. J. & Voas, R. B. (1991). The effect of license suspension upon DWI recidivism. *Alcohol, Drugs and Driving*, *7*(1), 43-54.

NHTSA. (1992). Model specifications for breath alcohol ignition interlock devices (BAIIDs). *57*, *Federal Register*, *67*, 11772-11787.

Project MATCH Research Group. (1997) Matching alcoholism treatments to client heterogeneity: Project Match posttreatment drinking outcomes, *Journal of Studies on Alcohol*, Vol. *58*, No. 1, 7-29.

Roth, R. (2006, June 19-21). *Plenary #1: Interlocks in New Mexico.* Paper presented at the International Technology Symposium, Mothers Against Drunk Driving (MADD), Albuquerque, NM.

Roth, R. (2009). Estimates of currently installed interlocks in the US. Sante Fe, NM: Impact DWI, Inc. Available at: http://www.impactdwi.org/2009currenlyinstalledinterloc ksbystate.pdf.

Roth, R., Voas, R. B. & Marques, P. R. (2007a). Mandating interlocks for fully suspended offenders: The New Mexico experience. *Traffic Injury Prevention*, *8*(1), 20-25.

Roth, R., Voas, R. B. & Marques, P. R. (2007b). Interlocks for first offenders: Effective? *Traffic Injury Prevention*, *8*(4), 346-352.

Roth, R., Voas, R. B. & Marques, P. R. (2009, in press). A note on the effectiveness of a house arrest alternative for motivating DWI offenders to install ignition interlocks. *Journal of Safety Research.*

Timken, D. & Marques, P. R. (2001a). *Support for Interlock Planning (SIP): Participants Workbook.* Calverton, MD: Pacific Institute for Research and Evaluation.

Timken, D. & Marques, P. R. (2001b). *Support for Interlock Planning (SIP): Providers Manual.* Calverton, MD: Pacific Institute for Research and Evaluation.

Voas, R. B., Blackman, K. O., Tippetts, A. S. & Marques, P. R. (2002). Evaluation of a program to motivate impaired driving offenders to install ignition interlocks. *Accident Analysis and Prevention*, *34*(4), 449-455.

Voas, R. B. & Marques, P. R. (1992). Model specifications for breath alcohol ignition interlock devices (BAIIDs). *The Federal Register*, *57*(67), 11772-11787.

Voas, R. B., Marques, P. R., Tippetts, A. S. & Beirness, D. J. (1999). The Alberta Interlock Program: The evaluation of a province-wide program on DUI recidivism. *Addiction*, *94*(12), 1849-1859.

Weisner, C., Matzger, H., Tam, T. & Schmidt, L. (2002). Who goes to alcohol and drug treatment? Understanding utilization with the context of insurance. *Journal of Studies on Alcohol and Drugs*, *63*(6), 673-682.

Wells-Parker, E., Bangert-Drowns, R., McMillen, R. & Williams, M. (1995). Final results from a meta-analysis of remedial interventions with drink/drive offenders. *Addiction*, *90*(7), 907-926.

Willis, C., Lybrand, S. & Bellamy, N. (2004). Alcohol ignition interlock programmes for reducing drink driving recidivism. *Cochran Database of Systematic Reviews*, *18*(4), CD004168.

In: Alcohol Ignition Interlock Programs
Editor: Elise B. Tiessart
ISBN: 978-1-62948-546-1

Chapter 2

IGNITION INTERLOCKS - WHAT YOU NEED TO KNOW: A TOOLKIT FOR POLICYMAKERS, HIGHWAY SAFETY PROFESSIONALS, AND ADVOCATES*

Karen Sprattler

ABSTRACT

The purpose of this alcohol ignition interlock toolkit is to provide information about alcohol ignition interlocks and their use to prevent impaired driving. Many States have legislation that requires an alcohol ignition interlock to be placed on the vehicles of Driving While Intoxicated (DWI) offenders.

The toolkit includes sections that address frequently asked questions about interlocks, cost and benefits of ignition interlock programs, research on ignition interlocks, point- counterpoint on ignition interlocks, talking points, and the current use of ignition interlocks by State. The toolkit also addresses issues to consider when putting together an ignition interlock program such as indigent funding, monitoring, and offender compliance.

---

* This is an edited, reformatted and augmented version of a National Highway Traffic Safety Administration publication, Report No. DOT HS 811 246 dated November 2009.

INTRODUCTION

Alcohol-impaired driving takes an enormous toll in the United States, killing approximately one person every 40 minutes. Despite continued efforts by enforcement, the judiciary, advocates and governmental agencies, nearly 13,000 people were killed in alcohol-impaired-driving crashes in 2007 (NHTSA 2008a). This number has remained remarkably stable for almost two decades after alcohol-involved fatalities declined significantly in the 1980s and early-to-mid 1990s. Many drivers involved in fatal alcohol-impaired-driving crashes have been arrested previously for driving while intoxicated (DWI). In 2007, drivers with a blood alcohol concentration (BAC) of .08 grams per deciliter or higher in fatal crashes were eight times more likely to have a prior conviction for driving while impaired than were drivers with no alcohol (NHTSA, 2008a).

The prevention of impaired driving is critical to reducing alcohol-impaired-driving deaths and injuries. More than 1.46 million drivers were arrested in the United States in 2006 for driving under the influence of alcohol or narcotics. This number represents an arrest rate of one DWI arrest for every 139 licensed drivers in the United States (NHTSA, 2008b).

Technology presents exciting possibilities in the area of impaired-driving prevention. One promising strategy is the breath alcohol ignition interlock device (BAIID). A BAIID, or more simply an ignition interlock, is an after-market technology device installed in a motor vehicle to prevent a driver from operating the vehicle if the driver has been drinking. Before starting the vehicle, a driver must breathe into the device and if the driver's BAG is over a pre-set limit, the ignition interlock will not allow the vehicle to start.

Research shows that ignition interlocks reduce recidivism among both first-time and repeat DWI offenders, with reductions in subsequent DWI arrests ranging from 50 to 90 percent while the interlock is installed on the vehicle (Voas & Marques, 2003; Willis et al., 2005; Vezina, 2002; Tippetts & Voas, 1997; Coben & Larkin, 1999). Forty-seven States and the District of Columbia currently allow the use of alcohol ignition interlocks for at least some DWI offenders; only Alabama, South Dakota, and Vermont do not. Some States mandate ignition interlock use; in others, judges, State administrators or even the offenders themselves choose whether or not to apply this promising sanction. Seven States mandate the use of ignition interlocks for all offenders; 22 mandate use for repeat offenders. However, although approximately 1.4 million DWI arrests are made each year, the most recent national estimate reports only 146,000 alcohol ignition interlocks are currently in use with impaired driving offenders (Roth, 2008a). Additional information about alcohol ignition interlock technology is needed by State and community decision and policy makers to establish usage levels that correspond with the potential of this technology to save lives. This Tool Kit brings together resources that explain and support the use of alcohol ignition interlocks, identifies issues faced by ignition interlock programs and includes information about the current use of the technology in each State and the District of Columbia. By preventing impaired drivers from starting and operating motor vehicles, the separation of an unsafe driver from a vehicle that has the potential to be a deadly weapon may prevent untold tragedy. This Tool Kit will advance the understanding of ignition interlock technology, improving its application as an effective strategy to save lives and prevent impaired driving.

FREQUENTLY ASKED QUESTIONS

Q: *What is an ignition interlock?*

A: An ignition interlock is a breath alcohol analyzer connected to the ignition of a car. A vehicle equipped with an ignition interlock cannot be driven unless the driver passes the unit's breath alcohol tests (National Interlock Service Web site, 2009).

Q: *How do offenders get an ignition interlock?*

A: Some State ignition interlock programs are administrative, managed by Departments of Motor Vehicles. Others are judicial, managed by courts and probation departments. Generally, ignition interlocks can be provided or required in one of four ways (NHTSA, 2007):

1) Required by individual judges as a condition of probation for some offenders;
2) As a voluntary option for some offenders in return for shorter license suspension;
3) Required by State law for some or all repeat offenders as a condition of license reinstatement; or
4) Required by State law for all offenders as a condition of license reinstatement.

Q: *How effective is an ignition interlock?*

A: Research shows that ignition interlocks are associated with substantial reductions in recidivism, ranging from 50 percent to 90 percent while the interlock is installed on the vehicle. These results come from several peer-reviewed studies and a meta-analysis examining the effectiveness of interlocks (Voas & Marques, 2003; Willis et al., 2005; Vezina, 2002; Tippetts & Voas, 1997; Coben & Larkin, 1999).

Q: *Are ignition interlocks effective with first-time and repeat DWI offenders?*

A: Yes. Research studies demonstrate that ignition interlocks are effective for both first-time and repeat DWI offenders. A research study in New Mexico (Voas et al., 2005) indicates that for first-time offenders with ignition interlocks, the rate of recidivism was 3.51 percent, while first-time offenders without ignition interlocks had a significantly higher re-arrest rate of 7.09 percent. Several research studies have been conducted with repeat DWI offenders and ignition interlocks. In one study of repeat DWI offenders in West Virginia (Tippetts & Voas, 1997), those with ignition interlocks had a recidivism rate of 1.6 percent while 6.4 percent of repeat offenders without ignition interlocks were re-arrested for DWI. Similar results were found in Maryland (Beck et al., 1999), when 2.4 percent of ignition interlocked repeat DWI offenders were re-arrested for alcohol-related traffic offenses, as compared to 6.7 percent of the repeat offenders who did not participate in the ignition interlock program.

Q: How reliable are ignition interlocks?

A: The NHTSA model specifications, which were adopted in 1992, provide that an ignition interlock must prevent a car from starting 90 percent of the time if the BAC is .01 g/dL greater than the preset limit (.02 g/dL in extreme weather conditions) (Mothers Against Drunk Driving [MADD], 2009).

Q: What happens if an offender takes medicine with an alcohol base or uses an alcohol-based mouthwash?

A: Alcohol is alcohol. If the BAC exceeds the pre-set level, the vehicle will not start. In the case of mouthwash, if the driver waits a few minutes for the mouth alcohol to dissipate, the driver should be able to start the vehicle (National Interlock Service Web site, 2009).

Q: What happens when an offender tries to start a vehicle after drinking alcohol?

A: The ignition interlock will enter a short lock-out period of a few minutes for the first failed BAG test and a longer lockout for any subsequent failed BAG test. This permits an opportunity for the alcohol to dissipate from the mouth and for the driver to consider the reason for the failed test (NIS, 2009).

Q: Are there ways an offender can bypass using an ignition interlock?

A: Gurrently available ignition interlocks have anti-circumvention features that prevent activities such as having others blow into the ignition interlock, or using a balloon or compressed air to blow into the ignition interlock. By using pressure and temperature sensors, recording all events related to vehicle use, and using running retests, many of the ways offenders have tried to circumvent ignition interlocks in the past have since been thwarted (MADD, 2009).

However, many offenders seek to circumvent ignition interlocks by claiming they do not need an ignition interlock because they do not intend to drive, they do not own vehicles, or they cannot provide sufficient breath samples. Some offenders fail to install ordered ignition interlocks or simply drive vehicles without ignition interlocks (Robertson et al., 2006).

Q: *What is a "running retest"?*

A: Many ignition interlocks require random, repeated breath tests once the vehicles have been started successfully. This reduces the likelihood that an "alcohol-free" bystander provided the breath test that allowed the vehicle to start, and it detects drivers with BAGs that are ascending after the vehicles are in motion. If a driver fails to provide a running retest or register a BAG in excess of the pre-set limit, either an auditory or visual warning or activation of an alarm will occur, alerting authorities. Manufacturers strongly recommend drivers not perform the running retest while the vehicle is in motion, but rather exit traffic and comply with the test (Robertson et al., 2006).

Q: *What happens when the ignition interlock is removed from the vehicle?*

A: Studies (Beirness, 2001; Beirness et al., 1998; Jones, 1993; Popkin et al., 1993; Goben & Larkin, 1999; Marques et al., 2001; DeYoung, 2002; Raub et al., 2003) have shown that ignition interlocks reduce recidivism from 50 to 90 percent while installed on vehicles. After the ignition interlock is removed, rates of recidivism may return to pre- ignition interlock recidivism levels. However, it may be possible to greatly enhance ignition interlock effectiveness by lengthening the time use is required, more closely integrating ignition interlock use with alcohol misuse treatment, or requiring permanent ignition interlock use for the most serious offenders (MADD , 2009; NHTSA, 2007).

Q: *How much do ignition interlocks cost?*

A: Installation of an ignition interlock runs between \$100 and \$250; typical monthly costs (including installation insurance and basic fees) are estimated to run between \$65 and \$90. Daily costs are approximately equal to the cost of one to two alcoholic drinks per day, or \$2 to \$3 per day, and far less than the costs of incarceration or electronic monitoring (Marques, 2008a). Some jurisdictions offset some costs for indigent offenders.

IGNITION INTERLOCK COSTS

Planning, sufficient resources and coordination are required to implement effective ignition interlock programs. States have varying approaches to funding ignition interlock programs, generally using fees and surcharges paid by DWI offenders. Research estimates of interlock benefit/cost suggest a $3 benefit for first-time DWI offenders and a $4 to $7 benefit for other DWI offenders accruing for each dollar of program cost (Miller, 2005) (Roth et al., 2007).

Costs to the Offender

Installation of an ignition interlock runs between $100 and $250; typical monthly costs (including installation insurance and basic fees) are estimated to run between $65 and $90 (Marques, 2008a). Cost variations can be attributed to factors such as program size (economies can often be achieved with larger scale programs), geographic areas to be covered or even competition between vendors. Daily costs of an interlock sanction are approximately equal to the cost of one to two alcoholic drinks per day, or $2 to $3 each day, far less than the costs of incarceration or electronic monitoring (Marques, 2008a).

Many States have taken steps to address concerns that the cost of interlock sanctions acts as a barrier to offender implementation. About 20 States have devised ways to offset costs for indigent offenders. Interlock indigent funds operate in many States. Some set up with fees from other offenders; other States provide funds through arrangements with interlock providers.

Costs to the State

Program administration costs vary with the design of each ignition interlock program. States with mandatory versus discretionary ignition interlock sanctions, or first-time versus repeat-offender interlock programs will differ in level of resources needed. States choosing to monitor interlock data on individual offender BAC tests and driving habits will incur greater costs than States that do not. Programs that mandate offender appearance before a court or administrative body for elevated BAC tests will incur greater costs than programs that let the immediate inability to drive serve as the offender's sanction for an elevated test.

As courts and administrative agencies struggle to provide services in a challenging economy, there is no simple solution as workloads increase and budgets tighten. From simple to complex, ignition interlock programs must balance the costs of program elements with how they can be funded. A few States impose additional monitoring fees on offenders to offset increased administrative costs, while some experts suggest using revenues from alcohol taxes or insurance surcharges to fund interlock programs.

Benefits of Ignition Interlock Programs

No highway safety improvement strategy is ever a silver bullet, but significant progress can be achieved through the application of effective countermeasures. Ignition interlock technology prevents alcohol-impaired driving by DWI offenders, resulting in increased public safety for all motorists, including the offender. Other benefits of ignition interlock programs include:

A Reduction in DWI Recidivism

Ignition interlock technology offers great promise in reducing subsequent drinking and driving behavior by DWI offenders. Research shows that ignition interlocks, while installed on an offender's vehicle, reduce recidivism among both first-time and repeat DWI offenders. More than 10 evaluations of ignition interlock programs have reported reductions in recidivism ranging from 50 to 90 percent, with an average reduction of 64 percent while the interlock is installed on the vehicle (Voas & Marques, 2003; Willis et al., 2005; Vezina, 2002; Tippetts & Voas, 1997; Coben & Larkin, 1999).

Legal Driving Status

When a DWI offender installs an ignition interlock, the offender regains legal driving status, either through provisional or full licensure. Legal driving status enables offenders to maintain employment, complete substance abuse treatment and take care of familial and court-ordered responsibilities that require driving. This is particularly important in rural areas where offenders may not have access to public transportation alternatives.

Offenders and Their Families Approve

Surveys of New Mexico DWI offenders found that 85 percent of those surveyed thought an ignition interlock sanction was fair to DWI offenders; 87

percent felt ignition interlocks reduced driving after drinking (Roth 2005,). A study conducted in the United Kingdom reported families of offenders with ignition interlocks were particularly in favor of this technology. Family members found ignition interlocks provided a level of reassurance that the offender was not driving while impaired and reported a generally positive experience and impact on their loved one's drinking habits (Beirness et al., 2007).

A Predictor of Future DWI Behavior

The record of breath tests logged into an ignition interlock has been found to be an excellent predictor of future DWI recidivism risk. Offenders with higher rates of failed BAC tests have higher rates of post-ignition interlock recidivism (Marques, 2008a).

In addition, the 20 to 30 percent of DWI offenders with the highest rates of elevated ignition interlock BAC tests also exhibit significantly higher levels of several different alcohol biomarkers, most of which are associated with problem drinking levels (Marques, 2008c). Experts suggest this BAC test data could provide critical information in the driver license restoration decision (Marques, 2008c).

Ignition Interlocks and Substance Abuse Treatment

Ignition interlocks effectively restrict an offender's driving privileges while giving the offender an opportunity to learn how alcohol consumption affects behavior (Beirness, 2001). Substance abuse treatment, a common requirement for DWI offenders, can be an extended process with setbacks and relapses.

An ignition interlock provides a safety net to greatly reduce the possibility that such setbacks result in impaired driving (Beirness et al., 1998). Experts believe a greater tie between ignition interlock sanctions and substance abuse treatment should be encouraged, as the integration of the two strategies mutually reinforce the likelihood of a reduction in an offender's impaired driving.

Cost-Effectiveness of Ignition Interlocks

Offenders ordered to install an ignition interlock find the daily costs to be comparable to the price of one to two alcoholic drinks, or $2 to $3 per day. Initial installation of the technology runs between $100 and $250 and monthly costs are between $65 and $90 (Marques, 2008a). Ignition interlock costs are far less than the costs of incarceration or electronic monitoring. Research shows that the public saves $3 to $7 for every $1 spent on ignition interlock devices for DWI offenders (Miller, 2005).

RESEARCH ON IGNITION INTERLOCK DEVICES

Numerous research efforts exploring the effectiveness of ignition interlocks as a sanction for DWI offenders have been conducted over the past 20 years. The research has been reasonably consistent in reporting 50- to 90-percent reductions in subsequent DWI recidivism when offenders have installed ignition interlocks on their vehicles (Voas & Marques, 2003; Willis et al., 2005; Vezina, 2002; Tippetts & Voas, 1997; Coben & Larkin, 1999).

Strengths of this research include highly comparable findings between studies, efforts examining a range of offender statuses and populations, sufficient sample sizes, international research, evaluations of both court-based and administrative programs and meta-analyses comparing results across research studies (TIRF, 2009).

Limitations of this research, noted across many of these studies, include a lack of randomly selected comparison groups as well as selection biases attributable to judicial discretion and the self-selective circumstances of most interlocked offenders. While the research on ignition interlocks is promising, these limitations must be taken into account when making program or policy decisions based upon this data (TIRF, 2009).

Ignition Interlock Effects on DWI Recidivism

- Research shows that alcohol interlocks reduce recidivism among both first-time and repeat offenders, including “hardcore” offenders—those offenders who repeatedly drive after drinking with high Blood Alcohol Concentrations (BACs) and are resistant to changing this behavior (Beirness et al. 1998., Coben & Larkin 1999, EMT Group 1990; Popkin et al., 1992; Morse & Elliot, 1992; Jones, 1993; Weinrath, 1997).

- More than 10 evaluations of interlock applications have demonstrated reductions in recidivism ranging from 50 to 90 percent while the interlock is installed on the vehicle (Voas & Marques, 2003; Willis et al., 2005; Vezina, 2002; Tippetts & Voas, 1997; Coben & Larkin, 1999).
- Once ignition interlocks are removed from vehicles, recidivism rates of ignition interlock users are similar to the rates for offenders who did not install ignition interlocks (Beirness, 2001; Beirness et al., 1998; Jones 1993; Popkin et al., 1993; Coben & Larkin, 1999; Marques et al., 2001; DeYoung, 2002; Raub et al., 2003).

Ignition Interlocks and First-Time DWI Offenders

Four studies (EMT Group 1990; Morse & Elliot 1992; Tippets & Voas, 1998; Voas et al., 1999) with unique offender populations, different measures of recidivism, and varying evaluation periods concluded that ignition interlock devices are effective in reducing recidivism in first-time DWI offenders. Findings include:

- A 2004 study of New Mexico's interlock program (Voas et al., 2005) compared a group of 862 offenders court-ordered to install interlocks with a group of 11,973 non-interlocked offenders. The study found interlocked offenders had a recidivism rate of 3.51 percent per year, compared to the non-interlocked group's rate of 7.09 percent, a 50-percent reduction in recidivism while the interlock was installed on the vehicle.
- An Alberta, Canada (Voas et al., 1999), study compared interlocked first offenders to control groups of reinstated and non-interlocked drivers. Measured against reinstated drivers, recidivism by interlocked first offenders was reduced by 89 percent; when compared to non-interlocked drivers, recidivism was reduced by 95 percent while the interlock was installed on the vehicle.

Ignition Interlocks and Repeat Offenders

Five studies involving repeat DWI offenders (EMT Group, 1990; Popkin et al., 1992; Morse & Elliot, 1992; Jones, 1993; Weinrath, 1997) have found that ignition interlocks are one of the most promising strategies available to prevent subsequent DWI behavior by these offenders. Research findings include:

- A study in Maryland (Beck et al., 1999) examined 1,387 repeat offenders who were eligible for license reinstatement. Half of the offenders were randomly assigned to receive an ignition interlock, the other half received no intervention. Participation in the interlock program reduced the risk of recidivism by almost 65 percent in the first year of the program, with an interlocked offender recidivism rate of 2.4 percent, compared to a non-interlocked offender rate of 6.7 percent while the interlock was installed on the vehicle.
- An Illinois study (Raub et al., 2003) looked at two similarly sized groups of repeat offenders who received restricted driving permits. One group was required to install ignition interlock devices, the second was not. After one year, interlocked offenders had a recidivism rate of 1.3 percent, compared to the non-interlocked recidivism rate of 8.7 percent—a reduction of 85 percent. Study authors also noted once interlocks were removed from the vehicles of the repeat offenders, there was a rapid return to pre-device recidivism rates.
- Numerous studies (Beirness, 2001; Beirness et al., 1998; Jones 1993; Popkin et al., 1993; Coben & Larkin, 1999; Marques et al., 2001; DeYoung, 2002; Raub et al., 2003) demonstrate ignition interlocks have a beneficial impact on recidivism *for as long as the device is installed in the vehicle*. Because of increased recidivism rates following removal of the device, several studies have reported that employing interlocks may be necessary as a long-term or permanent condition of driving for repeat offenders.

Ignition Interlock Effects on Crashes

The real threat associated with DWI behavior is the increased risk of alcohol-related crashes. Nearly all ignition interlock studies to date have examined DWI recidivism as a proxy measure for an interlock safety benefit. Once a larger number of these devices are in use, the data necessary to conclusively study the impact of ignition interlock devices on reducing alcohol-related crashes can be measured. At present, only one preliminary study in New Mexico has been able to examine this effect directly (Roth, 2008b).

- Preliminary results in New Mexico show an approximate 32-percent reduction in alcohol injury crashes for the years 2002–2006, a time period when interlock installation rates approached 35 percent of all arrested offenders. While a direct causal tie cannot be established, the evidence is persuasive.

Ignition Interlocks—Other Findings

Each attempt—successful or not—to use an interlocked vehicle generates data that is collected and stored by the ignition interlock device. This data is reviewed and used in some jurisdictions to monitor the interlock experience of DWI offenders. Through study of this data, researchers have made the following observations:

- Once the device is installed, offenders often try to circumvent the interlock in the first few weeks by tampering with breath samples and attempting to disengage the device. Tampering rates decrease over time as offenders recognize the futility of trying to circumvent the technology (Beirness et al., 2007).
- A high rate of breath test warnings/failures, particularly in the early morning, is a good predictor of DWI recidivism (Marques et al., 2003; Beirness & Marques, 2004).
- Several variables, but primarily more prior DWIs and more interlock warnings/ failures in the first five months of interlock usage predict more than 60 percent of recidivism, with a false positive rate of less than 10 percent (Marques et al., 2001).
- The 20–30 percent of DWI offenders with the highest rates of interlock warning/ failure also exhibit significantly higher levels of several different alcohol biomarkers from blood, hair or urine, most of which are associated with problem drinking levels. (Marques, 2008b).

Future Ignition Interlock Research

While numerous evaluations of ignition interlock effectiveness have been completed, work in additional interlock-related areas is necessary to optimize the use of this technology and appropriate use of the sanction. Experts have identified the following areas as important for continuing research:

- Determining the optimal structure for interlock programs (Beirness et al., 2003)
- The role of monitoring in interlock programs (TIRF, 2009)
- The interaction between interlocks and alcohol treatment (Beirness et al., 2003)
- Process evaluations of interlock programs (Coben & Larkin, 1999; Beirness et al., 2003)
- Outcome evaluations of interlock programs (Coben & Larkin, 1999)
- Examining the impact of ignition interlocks on the use of other sanctions for DWI offenders (i.e., are ignition interlocks becoming used more often in lieu of other sanctions?)

Other Considerations for Ignition Interlock Programs

Alcohol-impaired driving is a complex behavior that defies easy solutions. Each State defines these crimes and their sanctions differently, and responds with varying administrative and judicial sanctions. While ignition interlock technology offers great promise for reducing DWI behavior, creating an effective program within existing State systems can present challenges. As States consider instituting or upgrading ignition interlock policies or programs, a number of issues merit consideration by policy makers.

Program Considerations

Program Focus

What is a State's philosophical basis for an ignition interlock sanction? Is it public safety whereby an interlock is a protective shield to reduce the public's exposure to impaired drivers? Or is it a means of rehabilitation where interlocks detect and prevent driving by individual DWI offenders who continue to drink alcohol—or is it something in between? Answering these questions will inform interlock policies that speak to criteria for program participation, interlock noncompliance, length of interlock installation and more.

Indigent Funding

Many offenders ordered to install ignition interlocks claim they are unable to do so because of reduced financial capacity. A number of States have responded to this situation by creating a fund that will pay all or a portion of the costs of installing and maintaining the interlocks. In some States indigent funds are set up with fees paid by offenders; in other States a percentage of sales from providers support this fund. If States choose to make funds available to indigents, it is suggested that objective criteria for eligibility be developed to insure fair access to these resources.

Interlock Vendors

From a State perspective, how are vendors of interlock technology best managed? Several variations of management models exist, with strengths and challenges to each. Free market considerations favor multiple providers; management burden may favor fewer or even a sole provider so vendors can be more easily organized. States with rural populations need to consider the geographic distribution of vendors so all offenders can be served. In any case, the State should develop a common set of reporting protocols so authorities can compare interlock data across vendors, track the number of interlocks installed in offenders' vehicles and monitor the provision of interlock services by all vendors (Voas & Marques, 2007).

Technology Choices

When deciding which ignition interlock models will be approved for operating within a State, policy makers must thoroughly review and prioritize the range of technology options available. Interlock manufacturers offer a variety of products with an ever-increasing number of features available that affect the performance, tamper-resistance, and cost of the ignition interlock technology.

Monitoring and Reporting

Most ignition interlocks collect and record a wealth of information each time the interlock is accessed. Data related to vehicle use, driver alcohol use, and attempts to circumvent the technology can provide important information for driver control authorities. Monitoring this information and using it to direct offender behavior is critical to improving public safety. States must decide the frequency with which offenders download data from their interlocks to a service provider; decisions should also be made about how often vendors provide authorities with data and in what form it is delivered. Many experts believe governmental authorities are in a better position to interpret interlock data than vendors. Requiring vendors to report offender non-compliance when removal of an offender's interlock privilege could be an outcome of that non-compliance may set up a conflict of interest situation for vendors.

Some experts suggest setting varying offender monitoring parameters (e.g., content and frequency of reporting requirements), basing requirements upon the level of offender and their perceived risk. Monitoring ignition interlock data can be a very important method for the responsible authority to check on the performance of an offender. Most importantly, States must ensure the existence of adequate funding to enable court or administrative monitoring of data generated by offender interlock use.

Offender Compliance

Issues with offender compliance fall into three categories: (1) whether or not an offender installs an ordered interlock, (2) whether or not an offender chooses to participate in an interlock program, or (3) the degree to which an offender lives within the restrictions of the installed technology (Marques, 2008c; Marques, 2008a).

Successfully Installing an Interlock

In typical court mandated interlock programs, two-thirds of offenders still do not install ignition interlocks (Marques, 2008c). The risk of detection for driving-while-suspended violations is low and many offenders choose to drive without a license rather than install an interlock. Installation compliance can be improved with offender monitoring by program authorities and by making interlock installation the most attractive alternative for the offender. This means offering offenders the interlock option instead of more restrictive and expensive sanctions like electronically monitored "house arrest" or alcohol transdermal monitoring (Secure Continuous Remote Alcohol Monitor or SCRAM). For offenders who avoid interlock imposition by claiming no vehicle or that they will refrain from driving during periods of suspension, it may be necessary to sentence these offenders to the less–desirable sanctions to prevent illegal driving.

Choosing to Participate

In States where offenders have a choice in whether to participate in an interlock program, motivation to install an interlock is often weak. However, States that offer interlocks as the most appealing alternative—rather than electronically monitored "house arrest" or alcohol trans-dermal monitoring, have greater success with offenders choosing to install interlocks. Other interlock compliance incentives suggested by researchers include reduced fines, waiving/reducing insurance surcharges, or reductions in the length of hard driver license suspension.

When an Offender Tries to Drive after Drinking

The consequences for an offender who provides an elevated interlock BAC test vary greatly from State to State. Extremes range from no response because authorities do not monitor the offender interlock data generated by the technology to a very strong response—one or two elevated tests are grounds for removal from the interlock program. Some State programs simply conclude an interlock sanction is successful when it prevents the driver from driving after drinking. Other programs expect interlocks to monitor offender abstinence, a role interlock experts believe is not appropriate for the technology. States must consider the outcome they are ultimately seeking: if protection of the public is the goal, the immediate denial of an offender's ability to drive may be sanction enough for an elevated test. If the interlock is viewed as a tool to induce sobriety for an individual offender, elevated tests may demand further sanctions.

Research has found 60 to 80 percent of interlocks log positive BAG tests—most occurring in the morning, even though the majority of all tests occur between 4 and 6 p.m. (Marques et al., 2001). Experts believe most of the morning alcohol-positive tests are completed by drivers who drank heavily the night before and discover the realities of alcohol dissipation curves. Many experts suggest that after an initial "learning period," most offenders discover how to successfully drive within the parameters of the interlock (Beirness et al., 2007). Many drivers circumvent interlock sanctions by driving non-interlocked vehicles. Experts suggest States consider penalties for this type of circumvention that are equal to or greater than Driving After Suspension or Revocation charges. Some States are considering setting vehicle usage criteria when offenders are ordered to install an ignition interlock; legal sanctions could then be brought to bear on an offender who does not drive the interlocked vehicle. Flexibility is recommended in setting and extending interlock time requirements when offenders do not comply with interlock sanctions. Reasons for extending a period of interlock installation might include skipped tests, failed retests, circumventions, or a pattern of elevated BAG tests. Removal criterion should be based upon some period of alcohol-free driving; additional interlock time should be considered for subsequent DWI arrests.

Other Considerations

Stakeholder Involvement

As States consider implementing or improving ignition interlock programs, it is important to involve stakeholders in the process. Advisory committees or implementation work groups comprised of law enforcement, judges, prosecutors, State licensing administrators and treatment professionals can be critical in creating an effective interlock program. Once created, educational programs explaining the interlock program and technology for State agencies, the criminal justice system and the public will promote understanding and acceptance of this important sanction.

It is essential that law enforcement officials can easily identify offenders who are sentenced to drive interlocked vehicles. States should consider penalties for offenders who drive non-interlocked vehicles as well as note the interlock status on an offender's driver license for the benefit of law enforcement and other authorities.

Ignition Interlocks and Substance Abuse Treatment

Ignition interlocks have great potential to change the behavior of drivers who continue to combine drinking and driving. Interlocks can serve as a nexus between criminal justice system sanctions and substance abuse treatment by restricting offender's driving privileges while giving them the opportunity to learn how alcohol consumption affects behavior (Beirness, 2001). The ignition interlock should be incorporated into a comprehensive offender rehabilitation program to reduce the likelihood of recidivism once the interlock is removed (Beirness et al., 1998).

POINT – COUNTERPOINT

Point: Ignition interlocks reduce recidivism for first-time and repeat DWI offenders.

Counterpoint: Once the ignition interlock is removed from an offender's vehicle, rates of recidivism may return to pre- ignition interlock levels.

Commentary:

In a perfect world, the imposition of an ignition interlock would create a permanent change in the drinking and driving behavior of a DWI offender. In reality, many in the highway safety community are satisfied with the ignition interlock's "incapacitating" effect that prevents alcohol-impaired driving during the period of installation. During the installation period, ignition interlocks appear to help some offenders make changes in their long term drinking and driving behavior. For others, the sanction ceases to be effective when the ignition interlock is removed. Research is not clear as to the optimal length of ignition interlock period necessary to maximize behavior change (Marques, 2008a).

Many believe that, if the length of the period were increased and/or if ignition interlock use were combined with close supervision and/or substance abuse treatment, then the benefits would endure (Marques, 2008a).

Point: Offenders have concerns about installing an ignition interlock on their vehicle. Concerns cited include social embarrassment, family inconvenience, long warm-up times, and frequency of "rolling retests."

Counterpoint: Offenders ordered to install ignition interlocks are able to drive legally when using the technology, often sooner than if the offender did not install an ignition interlock.

Commentary:

With an ignition interlock installed, DWI offenders can maintain employment, attend school, get treatment, and take care of family obligations—yet are prevented from driving if alcohol has been used. Offenders and their families benefit because they are not faced with the same transportation, financial, and legal consequences as offenders who choose not to install ignition interlocks (Robertson et al., 2006).

Point: Across the United States, installation rates of ignition interlocks are low.

Counterpoint: In most States, offenders lack incentives for choosing ignition interlocks.

Commentary:

Many reasons account for low ignition interlock installation rates: uneven application of the sanction, offenders claim they do not own a vehicle or they say they will not drive during a license suspension or revocation. Other offenders simply fail to follow through on the ignition interlock installation or drive vehicles without ignition interlocks installed. Close supervision can help to close some of these loopholes. The often long delay between licensing action and required ignition interlock installation teaches many DWI offenders that they do not need a license to drive. Research is clear (Baker et al., 2002; Marques et al., 2003a, 2003b) that the majority of offenders (perhaps as many as 75% of them) continue to drive after license suspension, at least on occasion, and many continue to drink and drive. For ignition interlock programs to be successful, the installation of an ignition interlock must offer offenders a more attractive or less intrusive alternative to driving unlicensed or driving after drinking (Robertson et al., 2006).

> *Point*: Ignition interlocks should be court-ordered.
> *Counterpoint:* Ignition interlocks should be administrative sanctions.

Commentary:

Benefits and challenges exist in each type of program. Courts more often offer mechanisms to provide monitoring and follow-up through probation or court services, but engaging the many members of the judiciary and developing a common practice of ignition interlock imposition can be difficult. Administrative programs often offer more consistent application of ignition interlock sanctions and involve fewer people, which can make program management more efficient. However, administrative bodies typically possess less leverage with drivers than courts do to encourage program compliance. Twenty-one States operate court-based ignition interlock programs, eight run administrative programs and 19 States use a combination of judicial and administrative implementation of their ignition interlock programs.

> *Point*: Ignition interlocks provide a monitoring system in which trying to start a vehicle after drinking produces an immediate sanction for the offender– the inability to start a vehicle.
>
> *Counterpoint:* Interlocks may reduce drinking and driving even though they may not change the quantity an offender drinks.

Commentary:

Sanctions for impaired drivers often must balance the competing interests of public safety and individual sobriety. Ignition interlocks protect the public safety for other road users while offenders learn to separate driving from drinking. In cases where courts require offenders to abstain from alcohol, ignition interlocks can provide information to the courts about attempted drinking and driving behavior, but ignition interlocks are not designed to serve as an abstinence monitoring tool. Other technologies, such as home monitoring or transdermal alcohol monitoring devices (e.g., SCRAM) are better suited to monitor offender abstinence (Marques, 2008a).

Point: Some States require ignition interlock installation soon after arrest or conviction for the DWI offense.

Counterpoint: Some States require ignition interlock usage only upon reinstatement of driving privileges.

Commentary:

Deterrence theory suggests the sooner a sanction is imposed, the more likely it will be effective. Some States are reducing hard license revocation periods when an ignition interlock device is installed, believing public safety is increased during a time when many DWI offenders continue to drive, despite license suspension or revocation. If over time offenders learn they can drive undetected during revocation periods, there is little incentive to re-enter the licensing control system and install an ignition interlock in order to regain legal driving privileges.

MEDIA TALKING POINTS

Overview

Ignition interlock technology is a promising tool in the fight against alcohol-impaired driving. Using technology that stops a drinking driver from starting a motor vehicle, the acts of drinking and driving are effectively separated. This improvement in public safety benefits all motorists sharing the roadway. Most States have enacted laws that mandate or allow ignition interlocks as a sanction for DWI offenders; many are considering upgrades or improvements to existing laws.

Talking Points

- Ignition interlocks stop DWI offenders from driving after drinking.
  - Research is clear—for the period when ignition interlocks are installed on an offender's vehicle, rates of DWI recidivism are reduced an average of 64 percent (Voas & Marques, 2003; Willis et al., 2005; Vezina, 2002; Tippetts & Voas, 1997; Coben & Larkin, 1999).
  - The safety of the motoring public is protected—a drinking driver cannot drive a vehicle when an interlock is installed.
  - When surveyed, 85 percent of New Mexico DWI offenders thought ignition interlocks were fair to DWI offenders; 87 percent felt ignition interlocks reduced driving after drinking (Roth, 2005, in Robertson et al., 2006).
- Ignition interlocks allow offenders to drive legally to work, school, chemical addiction treatment and to take care of family obligations.
  - Research finds up to 75 percent of offenders drive illegally after a DWI arrest and license suspension (Baker et al., 2002; Marques et al., 2003a, 2003b).
  - Ignition interlocks give offenders a way to regain legal driving privileges while ensuring they drive alcohol-free.
  - The inability to drive legally can be a serious barrier to maintaining employment and completing substance abuse treatment, especially in areas lacking public transportation alternatives.
  - Ignition interlocks allow offenders to take care of family and court-ordered responsibilities.
- Ignition interlocks are a cost-effective sanction for DWI offenders.
  - Ignition interlock costs are borne by the offenders: installation of an ignition interlock runs between $100 and $250 and typical monthly costs are between $65 and $90 (Marques, 2008a).
  - Daily costs are approximately equal to the cost of one to two alcoholic drinks per day, or $2 to $3 per day, and far less than the costs of incarceration or electronic monitoring (Marques, 2008a).
  - Research shows that the public saves $3 to $7 for every $1 spent on ignition interlock devices for DWI offenders (Miller, 2005)

APPENDIX. CURRENT USE OF THE TECHNOLOGY

State*	Interlocks Mandatory Y/N	Law Passed	Administrative /Judicial	DWI Offender(s) Eligible	Indigent Fund Y/N	Interlocks In Use 2008***	2007 DWI Arrests (FBI UCR Data)**	Interlock Manufacturers Approved to Provide Services	State Contact
Alabama						4	12,851		
Alaska	Y	(6/08)	Judicial	Mandatory for all offenders	N	41	5,181	Draeger, SmartStart	Deputy Commissioner, AK Dept. of Corrections, 901-465-4610
Arizona	Y	(5/01)	Administrative	Mandatory for all offenders	N	6,849	38,260	Alcohol Detection Systems, Consumer Safety Technology, Draeger, Guardian, LifeSafer, SmartStart	Criminal Justice Liaison, Ignition Interlock Program Manager, Motor Vehicle Division, AZ DOT, 602-112-1611
Arkansas	N		Both	Required for 1st, 2nd and 3rd time offenders seeking restricted licenses	N	1,366	8,892	Draeger, Guardian, LifeSafer, SmartStart	Manager, Driver Control, Office of Driver Services, AR Dept. of Finance and Administration, 501-682-1060
California	Y		Both	Mandatory for repeat DWI while DAR/S offenders; others permissive	N	5,904	204,015	Alco Alert Interlock, Alcohol Detection Systems, Autosense International, Consumer Safety Technology, Draeger, Guardian,	Manager, CA DMV Driver Licensing Policy Unit, 916-651-6211

State*	Interlocks Mandatory Y/N	Law Passed	Administrative /Judicial	DWI Offender(s) Eligible	Indigent Fund Y/N	Interlocks In Use 2008***	2007 DWI Arrests (FBI UCR Data)**	Interlock Manufacturers Approved to Provide Services	State Contact
								LifeSafer, SmartStart	
Colorado	Y	(4/08)	Administrative	Mandatory for repeat offenders; others permissive	Y	6,104	21,969	Alcohol Sensors International, AutoSense International, Combined Systems Technology, Draeger, Guardian, LifeSafer, SmartStart	Operations Director / Driver Control, CO Dept. of Revenue, 303-205-5195
Connecticut	N		Both	Repeat offenders	Y	335	8,511	Alcohol Detection Systems, Consumer Safety Technology, Draeger, SmartStart	Senior Assistant State's Attorney, Traffic Safety Resource Prosecutor, CT Division of Criminal Justice, 860-258-5926
Delaware	Y		Judicial	Mandatory for repeat offenders; others permissive	Y	83	229	Draeger, LifeSafer	Management Analyst, DE Office of Highway Safety, 302-612-1639
District of Columbia	N		Both	Repeat offenders	Y	-	23	No manufacturers have yet been approved	DMV Driver Services Administrator, 202-121-5450
Florida	V	(6/08)	Both	Mandatory for repeat, high (.15+) BAC, or offenders with a	N	6,138	58,824	Alcohol Countermeasure Systems, LifeSafer	Bureau of Driver Education & DUI Programs, Division of Driver Licenses, 850-

Appendix. (Continued)

State*	Interlocks Mandatory Y/N	Law Passed	Administrative /Judicial	DWI Offender(s) Eligible	Indigent Fund Y/N	Interlocks In Use 2008***	2007 DWI Arrests (FBI UCR Data)**	Interlock Manufacturers Approved to Provide Services	State Contact
				minor in vehicle; others permissive					611-3815
Georgia	V		Judicial	Mandatory for repeat offenders; others permissive	N	1,919	26,442	Alcohol Detection Systems, AutoSense International, Consumer Safety Technology, Determinator, Draeger, Guardian, LifeSafer, Safety Interlock Systems, SmartStart	Regulatory Compliance Division, GA Dept. Driver Services, 110-413-8413
Hawaii	V	(1/2010)	Both	Mandatory for repeat and high (.15+) BAC offenders; may change to all with 2009 Legislature	V	-	5,059*	TBD	Highway Safety Specialist, HI DOT, 808-581-6315
Idaho	V		Judicial	Mandatory for repeat offenders; others permissive	V	455	11,014	Consumer Safety Technology, Guardian, LifeSafer, SmartStart	Grants/Contract Officer, Office of Highway Operations and Safety, 208-334-4461
Illinois	V	(8/01)	Judicial	Mandatory for all	V	3,381	5,624	AAA Interlock,	Director BAIID &

State*	Interlocks Mandatory Y/N	Law Passed	Administrative /Judicial	DWI Offender(s) Eligible	Indigent Fund Y/N	Interlocks In Use 2008***	2007 DWI Arrests (FBI UCR Data)**	Interlock Manufacturers Approved to Provide Services	State Contact
				offenders				Alco- Test, Consumer Safety Technology, Guardian, National Interlock Systems, SmartStart	MDDP, 201 Howlett Bldg., Springfield, IL 62156, 211-182-4128
Indiana	N		Judicial	All offenders	N (Indigents do not have to pay; unclear who pays in this case)	182	23,463	Guardian, SmartStart	Traffic Safety Resource Prosecutor, 311-232-1836
Iowa	V		Both	Mandatory for all offenders with BAC of .10+ or involved in a crash	N	4,618	13,130	Autosense, Consumer Safety Technology, Draeger, Guardian, LifeSafer, SmartStart	Governor's Traffic Safety Bureau, IA DPS, 515-125-6128
Kansas	Y		Both	Mandatory for all but 1st offenders with BAC less than .15	Y	861	12,080	Autosense International, Consumer Safety Technology, Draeger, Guardian, LifeSafer, SmartStart	Chief, Driver Control Bureau, DMV, KS Dept. of Revenue, 185-296-6894
Kentucky	N		Judicial	Repeat offenders	N	252	3,490	Alcohol Sensor International, AutoSense	Court Record Section Supervisor, Div. of Driver Licensing,

Appendix. (Continued)

State*	Interlocks Mandatory Y/N	Law Passed	Administrative /Judicial	DWI Offender(s) Eligible	Indigent Fund Y/N	Interlocks In Use 2008***	2007 DWI Arrests (FBI UCR Data)**	Interlock Manufacturers Approved to Provide Services	State Contact
								International, Consumer Safety Technology, Draeger, Guardian, LifeSafer, SmartStart	Dept. of Vehicle Regulation, 502-564-0219 x 4205
Louisiana	Y	(1/01)	Judicial	Mandatory for all offenders	N	1,823	8,125	Alcohol Detection Systems, Consumer Safety Technology, Draeger, Guardian, LifeSafer, SmartStart	Driver Management Manager, Office of Motor Vehicles, LA DPS, 225-925-6983
Maine	N		Administrative	Repeat offenders	N	-	8,091	No devices have yet been approved by the State	Sr. Section Manager, Driver License Services, ME Bureau of Motor Vehicles, 201-624-9095
Maryland	N		Both	Repeat offenders and specific others	Y	5,966	24,230	Alcohol Detection Systems, Guardian, Draeger, National Interlock, SmartStart	Driver Programs, MD Motor Vehicle Administration, 410-424-3043
Massachusetts	Y		Both	Mandatory for repeat offenders seeking a hardship license; others permissive	N	2,186	11,146	Alcohol Detection Systems, Draeger, Guardian, LifeSafer, SmartStart	Executive Office of Transportation, Registry of Motor Vehicles, Interlock Compliance

State*	Interlocks Mandatory Y/N	Law Passed	Administrative /Judicial	DWI Offender(s) Eligible	Indigent Fund Y/N	Interlocks In Use 2008***	2007 DWI Arrests (FBI UCR Data)**	Interlock Manufacturers Approved to Provide Services	State Contact
									Department, 611-351-9119
Michigan	N		Judicial	Repeat offenders	Y (Low income offenders pay $1/day by law)	3,994	40,584	American Interlock, National Interlock Service, New Horizon Interlock, SmartStart	Ignition Interlock Coordinator, Driver Assessment and Appeal Division, MI Dept. of State, 511-335-0104
Minnesota	N		Administrative	All offenders	N	9	31,135	Consumer Safety Technology, Draeger, SmartStart	Alcohol Coordinator, Office of Traffic Safety, MN DPS, 651-201-1014
Mississippi	N		Judicial	Repeat offenders	N	52	7,881	LifeSafer	Section Chief, MS Crime Lab, 601-987-1600
Missouri	Y	(5/08)	Judicial	Mandatory for repeat offenders; others permissive	N	2,743	31,633	AutoSense Int'l., Consumer Safety Technology, Draeger, Guardian, Lifesafer, SmartStart	Sr. Systems Management Analyst, Highway Safety Division, MO DOT, 573-751-5960
Montana	N		Judicial	All offenders	N	136	3,264	Consumer Safety Technology, Guardian	Chief, Records and Driver Control Bureau, Motor Vehicle Division, 406-444-1776

Appendix. (Continued)

State*	Interlocks Mandatory Y/N	Law Passed	Administrative /Judicial	DWI Offender(s) Eligible	Indigent Fund Y/N	Interlocks In Use 2008***	2007 DWI Arrests (FBI UCR Data)**	Interlock Manufacturers Approved to Provide Services	State Contact
Nebraska	Y	(4/08)	Both	Mandatory for all offenders	N	1,030	12,350	Alcohol Detection Systems, Consumer Safety Technology, Draeger, Guardian, LifeSafer, SmartStart	Legal Counsel, NE Dept. of Motor Vehicles, 402-471-4706
Nevada	Y		Judicial	Mandatory for high (.18+) BAC, fatal or serious injury crash, 3rd or more offenders seeking a restricted license; others permissive	N	405	12,538	Alcohol Detection System, Consumer Safety Technology, Draeger, Guardian, National Interlock System, SmartStart	Impaired Driving Programs Manager, Office of Highway Safety, NV DPS, 775-684-7477
New Hampshire	Y		Judicial	Mandatory for repeat DWI while DAR/S offenders immediately; aggravated and repeat offenders after period of revocation	N (Hardship credit funded by providers)	7	4,146	Consumer Safety Technology, Draeger	Administrator, Division of Motor Vehicles, NH Dept. of Safety, 603-271-0351
New Jersey	N		Judicial	All offenders	N	617	25,031	Alcohol Detection Systems, Draeger, Guardian, National	Motor Vehicle Commission, Interlock Bureau, NJ

State*	Interlocks Mandatory Y/N	Law Passed	Administrative /Judicial	DWI Offender(s) Eligible	Indigent Fund Y/N	Interlocks In Use 2008***	2007 DWI Arrests (FBI UCR Data)**	Interlock Manufacturers Approved to Provide Services	State Contact
								Interlock Service, SmartStart	DOT, 609-292-4630
New Mexico	Y	(6/05)	Both	Mandatory for all offenders	Y	8,133	10,006	Alcohol Countermeasure Systems, Alcohol Detection Systems, Consumer Safety Technology, Draeger, Guardian, LifeSafer, SmartStart	Ignition Interlock Program Manager, Traffic Safety Bureau, NM DOT, 505-795-2407
New York	Y		Judicial	Mandatory for high (.18+) BAC offenders; other repeat offenders permissive	N	1,276	28,440	Alcohol Detection Systems, Consumer Safety Technology, Draeger, Guardian, Interceptor Ignition Interlock, LifeSafer, SmartStart	NYS Dept. of Probation and Correctional Alternatives, 518-485-9941
North Carolina	Y		Both	Mandatory for repeat and high (.15+) BAC offenders seeking a hardship license; others permissive	N	8,003	26,928	Monitech	Chief Resource Prosecutor, NC Conference of District Attorneys, 919-890-1500
North Dakota	N		Both	All offenders	N	-	4,115	None approved to date	Manager, Traffic Safety Office, ND DOT, 701-328-4434

Appendix. (Continued)

State*	Interlocks Mandatory Y/N	Law Passed	Administrative /Judicial	DWI Offender(s) Eligible	Indigent Fund Y/N	Interlocks In Use 2008***	2007 DWI Arrests (FBI UCR Data)**	Interlock Manufacturers Approved to Provide Services	State Contact
Ohio	N		Judicial	All offenders	N	2,580	19,155	Alcohol Countermeasures System, Consumer Safety Technology, Draeger, Guardian, LifeSafer, SmartStart	OH DPS Legal Section, 614-752-7014
Oklahoma	N		Both	Repeat offenders reinstating a drivers license	N	1,722	18,229	Consumer Safety Technology, Draeger, Guardian, LifeSafer, SmartStart	Ignition Interlock Program Administrator, Board of Tests for Alcohol and Drug Influence, 405-425-2468
Oregon	Y		Both	Mandatory for all offenders seeking a hardship license; all at end of suspension	Y	1,651	17,096	Alco Alert Interlock, Consumer Safety Technology, Draeger, Guardian , LifeSafer, SmartStart	Driver Control Program Coordinator, OR DOT - DMV, 503-945-5276
Pennsylvania	Y		Administrative	Mandatory for repeat offenders	N	3,419	49,238	Alcohol Countermeasures Systems Corp., Alcohol Detection Systems, Consumer Safety Technology, Draeger, Guardian,	Manager of Alcohol Programs, PA DOT, 717-783-1902

State*	Interlocks Mandatory Y/N	Law Passed	Administrative /Judicial	DWI Offender(s) Eligible	Indigent Fund Y/N	Interlocks In Use 2008***	2007 DWI Arrests (FBI UCR Data)**	Interlock Manufacturers Approved to Provide Services	State Contact
								LifeSafer, SmartStart	
Rhode Island	N		Judicial	Repeat offenders	N	1	2,131	None approved to date	Supervisor, Breath Analysis Section, Forensic Sciences Laboratory, RI Dept. of Health
South Carolina	N	(5/08)	Judicial	Repeat offenders	Y	3	11,712	National Interlock Systems	Director, Program Development and Grants Management, SC Probation, Parole and Pardon Services, 803-734-2789
South Dakota						76	4,203		
Tennessee	Y		Both	Mandatory for 2nd in 5 years offender seeking a restricted license; permissive for others	N (May be paid from ADAT funds)	246	27,178	Consumer Safety Technologies, Draeger, SmartStart	TN Highway Patrol, TN Dept. of Safety, 615-687-2400
Texas	Y		Judicial	Mandatory for repeat and high (.15+) BAC offenders; others permissive	N (No indigent fund but providers will reduce costs for indigents)	14,395	88,236	Consumer Safety Technology, Draeger, Guardian, LifeSafer, SmartStart	TX Judicial Resource Liaison, 512-482-8986
Utah	N		Both	All offenders	N	1,311	7,204	Alcohol Sensors	Alcohol Program

Appendix. (Continued)

State*	Interlocks Mandatory Y/N	Law Passed	Administrative/ Judicial	DWI Offender(s) Eligible	Indigent Fund Y/N	Interlocks In Use 2008***	2007 DWI Arrests (FBI UCR Data)**	Interlock Manufacturers Approved to Provide Services	State Contact
					(No indigent fund, however court can order provider to absorb costs)			International, Consumer Safety Technology, Guardian, LifeSafer, SmartStart	Manager, Highway Safety Office, UT DPS, 801-957-8586
Vermont						2	3,662		
Virginia	Y	(3/08)	Administrative	Mandatory for repeat and high (.15+) BAC offenders; others permissive	N (No indigent fund, however court may waive or reduce fees for indigents)	4,253	24,170	Draeger	Executive Director, Commission on VASAP, 804-786-5895
Washington	Y	(3/08)	Both	Mandatory for all offenders	N	9,997	37,317	Autosense International, Consumer Safety Technology, Draeger, Guardian,	Impaired Driving Program Manager, WA Traffic Safety Commission, 360-725-9889

State*	Interlocks Mandatory Y/N	Law Passed	Administrative/ Judicial	DWI Offender(s) Eligible	Indigent Fund Y/N	Interlocks In Use 2008***	2007 DWI Arrests (FBI UCR Data)**	Interlock Manufacturers Approved to Provide Services	State Contact
								Lifesafer, SmartStart	
West Virginia	Y	(4/08)	Administrative	Mandatory for repeat offenders	Y	1,095	6,327	LifeSafer	Supervisor, DUI-Interlock Section, WV DMV, 304-558-1672
Wisconsin	Y		Judicial	Mandatory for 2nd in 5 years; other repeat offenders permissive	N	967	41,308	Consumer Safety Technology, Draeger, LifeSafer	Chief, Driver Information Section, WI DOT 608-264-7002
Wyoming	Y		Administrative	Mandatory for repeat and high (.15+) BAC offenders, test refusers	N	141	6,116	Consumer Safety Technology, SmartStart	Program Manager, WY DOT, 307-777-4815
Total						117,337****			

* State laws current as of May 2009

** 2006 FBI UCR data

*** Ignition interlock manufacturer SmartStart does not report devices in use by State. SmartStart reported 29,000 devices in use in the United States as of August 2008.

**** Total U.S. ignition interlock use 146,337 (Roth, 2008a).

REFERENCES

Baker, S. P., Braver, E. R., Chen, L-H., Li, G., & Williams, A. F. (2002). Drinking Histories of Fatally Injured Drivers. *Injury Prevention 8*(3), 221–226.

Beck, K., Rauch, W., Baker, E., & Williams, A. (1999). Effects of Ignition Interlock License Restrictions on Drivers with Multiple Alcohol Offenses: A Random Trial in Maryland. *American Journal of Public Health 89,* 1696–1700.

Beirness, D. J., Simpson, H. M., & Mayhew, D. R. (1998). Programs and Policies for Reducing Alcohol-Related Motor Vehicle Deaths and Injuries. *Contemporary Drug Problems 25,* 553–578.

Beirness, D. J. (2001). Best Practices for Alcohol Interlock Programs. Ottawa: Traffic Injury Research Foundation.

Beirness, D. J., Simpson, H. M., & Robertson, R.D. (2003). International Symposium on Enhancing the Effectiveness of Alcohol Ignition Interlock Programs. *Traffic Injury Prevention 4*(3), 179–182.

Beirness, D. J., & Marques, P. M. (2004). Alcohol Ignition Interlock Programs. *Traffic Injury Prevention 5*(3), 299–308.

Beirness, D. J., Clayton, A., & Vanlaar, W. G. M. (2007). An Investigation of the Usefulness, the Acceptability and Impact on Lifestyle of Alcohol Ignition Interlocks in Drink Driving Offenders.

Coben, J. H., & Larkin, G. L. (1999). Effectiveness of Ignition Interlock Devices in Reducing.

Drunk Driving Recidivism. *American Journal of Preventive Medicine 16,* 81–87.

DeYoung, D. J. (2002). An Evaluation of the Implementation of Ignition Interlock in California. *Journal of Safety Research 33,* 473–482.

EMT Group. (1990). Evaluation of the California Ignition Interlock Pilot Program for DWI Offenders (Farr-Davis Driver Safety Act of 1986). Prepared for The California Department of Alcohol and Drug Programs and The California Office of Traffic Safety. Sacramento, CA: The EMT Group, Inc.

Ignition Interlock FAQs. (2009, March). Mothers Against Drunk Driving. (http://www.madd.org).

Jones, B. (1993). The Effectiveness of Oregon's Ignition Interlock Program. In: H.D. Utzelmann, H. D., Berghaus, G., Kroj, G. (Eds.) Alcohol, Drugs and Traffic Safety—T-92: Proceedings of the 12th International Conference on Alcohol, Drugs and Traffic Safety, Köln, Germany, 28

September—2 October 1992. Köln: Verlage TÜV Rheinland GmbH, Vol. 3, pp. 1460–1465.

Marques, P. R., Tippetts, A. S., Voas, R. B., & Beirness, D. J. (2001). Predicting Repeat DWI Offenses with the Alcohol Interlock Recorder. *Accident Analysis and Prevention 33*(5), 609–619.

Marques, P. R., Tippetts, A. S., & Voas, R. B. (2003a). The Alcohol Interlock: An Underutilized Resource for Predicting and Controlling Drunk Drivers. *Traffic Injury Prevention 4*(3), 188–194.

Marques, P. R., Tippetts, A. S., & Voas, R. B. (2003b). Comparative and Joint Prediction of DUI Recidivism from Alcohol Ignition Interlock and Driver Records. *Journal of Studies on Alcohol 64*(1), 83–92.

Marques, P. R., & Voas, R. B. (2008a, February). Alcohol Interlock Program Features Survey. Unpublished Survey Results from the Interlock Working Group of the International Council of Alcohol Drugs and Traffic Safety.

Marques, P. R. (2008b, March). Engaging and Educating Treatment Professionals and their System of Care. Presentation at the 9th Annual International Alcohol Interlock Symposium, Tallberg, Sweden 2008. (www.interlocksymposium.com/site/ywd_acs_corporation/assets/ pdf/PaulMarques_2008.pdf).

Marques, P. R. (2008c, October). "Alcohol Ignition Interlock Facts (and some evidence—based conjectures)." Calverton, MD: Pacific Institute for Research and Evaluation, pp. 1–4.

Miller, T. R., & Hendrie, D. (2005). How Should Governments Spend the Drug Prevention Dollar: A Buyer's Guide, in Stockwell, T., &Gruenewald, P., et al. (eds), *Preventing Harmful Substance Use: The Evidence Base for Policy and Practice*, West Sussex: John Wiley & Sons, 415–431.

Morse, B. J., & Elliott, D. S. (1992). Hamilton County Drinking and Driving Study. Interlock Evaluation: Two Year Findings. Boulder, CO: University of Colorado Institute of Behavioral Science.

NHTSA. (2007). Reducing Impaired-Driving Recidivism Using Advanced Vehicle-Based Alcohol Detection Systems: A Report to Congress. DOT HS 810 876. Washington, DC: National Highway Traffic Safety Administration, pp. 9–15.

NHTSA. (2008a). Traffic Safety Facts 2007: Alcohol-Impaired Driving. DOT HS 810 985. Washington, DC: National Highway Traffic Safety Administration.

NHTSA. (2008b). Traffic Safety Facts 2007: Overview. DOT HS 810 993. Washington, DC: National Highway Traffic Safety Administration.

National Interlock Service. (2009, March). Participant FAQ's. (www.nationalinterlock.com/ faq.asp)

Popkin, C. L., Stewart, J. R., Beckmeyer, J., & Martell, C. (1993). An Evaluation of the Effectiveness of Interlock Systems in Preventing DWI Recidivism Among Second-Time DWI Offenders. In: Utzelmann , H.D., Berghaus, G., & Kroj, G. (Eds.) Alcohol, Drugs and Traffic Safety—T-92: Proceedings of the 12th International Conference on Alcohol, Drugs and Traffic Safety, Köln, Germany, 28 September—2 October 1992. Köln: Verlage TÜV Rheinland GmbH, Vol. 3, pp. 1466–1470.

Raub, R. A., Lucke, R. E., & Wark, R. I. (2003). Breath Alcohol Ignition Interlock Devices: Controlling the Recidivist. *Traffic Injury Prevention 4,* 199–205.

Road Safety Research Report No. 88. London: Department for Transport.

Robertson, R. D., Vanlaar W. G. M., & Simpson, H. M. (2006). Ignition Interlocks From Research to Practice: A Primer for Judges. Ottawa: Traffic Injury Research Foundation.

Roth, R. (2005). Surveys of DWI Offenders Regarding Ignition Interlocks. Anonymous surveys conducted before Victim Impact Panels in Santa Fe and Albuquerque, NM. (Personal communication cited in Robertson, R. D., Vanlaar W. G. M., & Simpson, H. M. (2006). Ignition Interlocks From Research to Practice: A Primer for Judges. Ottawa: Traffic Injury Research Foundation.)

Roth, R., Voas, R., & Marques, P. (2007). Interlocks for First Offenders: Effective? *Traffic Injury Prevention 8,* 346–352.

Roth, R. (2008a, September). Estimates of Currently Installed Interlocks in the US. GHSA conference handout.

Roth, R. (2008b, March). New Mexico Interlock Program Overview. PowerPoint presentation 10-28-08, Drive Sober Illinois Web site. drivesoberillinois.org/pdf/Richard%20Roth.pdf.

Tippetts, A. S., & Voas, R. B. (1997). The Effectiveness of the West Virginia Interlock Program on Second Drunk-Driving Offenders. In: Mercier-Guyon, C. (Ed.) Alcohol, Drugs and Traffic Safety—T97. Proceedings of the 14th International Conference on Alcohol, Drugs and Traffic Safety, Annecy, France, September 21–26, 1997. Annecy: CERMT, Vol.1, pp. 185–192.

Tippets, A. S., & Voas, R. B. (1998). The Effectiveness of the West Virginia Interlock Program. *Journal of Traffic Medicine 26,* 19–24.

Traffic Injury Research Foundation (2009). Alcohol Interlock Curriculum: Research Summary. Curricula Research Summary, Ottawa: pp.1–43.

Vezina, L. (2002). The Quebec Alcohol Interlock Program: Impact on Recidivism and Crashes. In: Mayhew, D. R., & Dussault, C. (eds.) Alcohol, Drugs and Traffic Safety–T2002. Proceedings of the 16th International Conference on Alcohol, Drugs and Traffic Safety. Montreal, August 4–9, 2002. Quebec City: Societe de l'assurance automobile du Quebec, pp. 97–104.

Voas, R. B., Marques, P. R., Tippetts, A. S., & Beirness, D. J. (1999). The Alberta Interlock Program: The Evaluation of a Province-wide Program on DWI Recidivism. *Addiction 94*(12), 1849–1859.

Voas, R. B., & Marques, P. R. (2003). Commentary: Barriers to Interlock Implementation. *Traffic Injury Prevention 4*(3), 183–187.

Voas, R. B., Roth, R., & Marques, P.R. (2005). Interlocks for First Offenders: Effective? In: Robinson, R. D., Vanlaar, W. G. M., Beirness, D. J. (Eds.) Alcohol Interlock Programs: A Global Perspective. Proceedings of the 6th International Symposium on Alcohol Ignition Interlock Programs, Annceny, France, September 25–27, 2005. Ottawa: Traffic Injury Research Foundation, pp.7–8.

Voas, R. B., & Marques, P. R. (2007). History of Alcohol Vehicle Interlock Programs: Lost Opportunities and New Possibilities. Eighth Annual Ignition Interlock Symposium, Seattle, WA.

Weinrath, M. (1997). The Ignition Interlock Program for Drunk Drivers: A Multivariate Test. *Crime and Delinquency 43*(1), 42–59.

Willis, C., Lybrand, S., & Bellamy, N. (2005). Alcohol Ignition Interlock Programmes for Reducing Drink Driving Recidivism (Review). *The Cochrane Database of Systematic Reviews* (4).

INDEX

M

N

O

P

Q

R

S